MARSHALL LAW

THE LIFE & TIMES OF A
BALTIMORE BLACK PANTHER

MARSHALL "EDDIE" CONWAY
AND DOMINQUE STEVENSON

AK
PRESS
EDINBURGH · OAKLAND · BALTIMORE

Marshall Law:
The Life and Times of a Baltimore Black Panther
By Marshall "Eddie" Conway and Dominque Stevenson

© 2011 Marshall Conway & Dominque Stevenson

This edition © 2011 AK Press (Edinburgh, Oakland, Baltimore)

ISBN-13: 978-1-84935-022-8
Library of Congress Control Number: 2010925763

AK Press
674-A 23rd Street
Oakland, CA 94612
USA
www.akpress.org
akpress@akpress.org

AK Press UK
PO Box 12766
Edinburgh EH8 9YE
Scotland
www.akuk.com
ak@akdin.demon.co.uk

The above addresses would be delighted to provide you with the latest AK Press distribution catalog, which features several thousand books, pamphlets, zines, audio and video recordings, and gear, all published or distributed by AK Press. Alternately, visit our websites to browse the catalog and find out the latest news from the world of anarchist publishing:
www.akpress.org | www.akuk.com
revolutionbythebook.akpress.org

Cover by Margaret Killjoy | www.birdsbeforethestorm.net

Interior by Kate Khatib | www.manifestor.org/design

Printed in Canada on 100% recycled, acid-free paper with union labor.

Table of Contents

For the ancestors, Eleanor Conway and Wilhelmina Hayes, and the children.

Prologue

The Court: *Mr. Conway, I'm going to warn you right now on the record that unless you behave yourself...*

(The remainder of the Court's remarks inaudible because of the defendant's interruption.)

The Defendant: *Behave myself? I want an attorney of my choice. What you mean, why don't you behave yourself? You said I could have an attorney of my choice. I give you a name and you're going to tell me behave myself and give me somebody who you hope to participate in the railroad job.*

The Court: *Mr. Conway, would you allow me to make one statement? That is this—I'm formally advising you and warning you that if you persist in this conduct, the trial will go forward without you. You will remain outside of the courtroom.*

The Defendant: *The trial will go forward without me if you don't let me have an attorney of my choice. If you're going to give me an attorney that I don't desire to have on a homicide charge, then the trial will go forward without me, because I'm not going to participate in it, because I have an attorney of my choice, and you will not allow him to be here. So it's your trial.*

The Court: *All right. Now would you care to be seated, or do you wish to leave the courtroom?*

The Defendant: Right. I wish to leave the courtroom. (Holds hands up to be cuffed.) Look, the man asked me did I want to go. I want to go.

The Court: All right.

The Defendant: Look, I'm not going to be taking part in this madness.

"Hey Conway." I heard the floor supervisor say my name before I saw him. "Report to the supervisor's office ASAP."

I was working the night shift at the main post office in Baltimore, a stretch of time that spanned eleven at night to seven in the morning. It was 1970, but the work was still much like picking cotton: rows and rows of black faces tossing mail into boxes, while a white man stood by, supervising the whole process. Workers could talk to each other on the line as long as they kept the mail moving and met their quota, but they had to ask permission from the supervisor to go to the restroom. The workers who the supervisor identified as rebellious, who also happened to be mostly black, were placed in an area of the post office called parcel post. This is where I spent most of my time, and it was real grunt work—heavy boxes that required sorting before we tossed them into large hampers. It had always reminded me of the stories I had heard of the days when the more unruly black slaves were sold further south, where the labor and conditions were more strenuous.

It was because of conditions like these that some of us had begun to organize a union for black workers. We felt that the existing postal union wasn't representing our needs and concerns. I was a key organizer of the new union, and as I walked down the hall to the supervisor's office, I mentally prepared myself to step through his door and be read the riot act for my organizing work. As a member of the Black Panther Party, I had begun to expect these situations, but at that moment, I never could have foreseen the aggression that the government would employ to dismantle our movement. We were simply outgunned and outnumbered, just as I was at that moment when I walked into the office and found myself facing five white men with .38 caliber revolvers pointed directly at my chest. History holds true that this has never been a good situation for a man of African descent. I tried to maintain my cool as I scanned the room and sized up the situation, but as the men tightened the handcuffs around my wrists, I resigned myself to the fact that there was nothing I could do.

I initially thought that federal agents were abducting me because of my affiliation with the Black Panther Party, so I was determined to keep my wits about me while I tried to assess the situation. Most of us in the party leadership in Maryland had been aware of warrants for our arrest for various charges for at least the past six months. I had also become increasingly aware of the harassment and scare tactics that the government used to discredit and derail our efforts at organizing in our communities. Yet, I still didn't have a clue when these plainclothes officers took me to Central Booking at the Baltimore City Jail and charged me as an accessory to murder in the case of a "missing" informant.

So began what would become an odyssey of indeterminate time. After nearly four decades in Maryland prisons, if I walked out tomorrow it would not end there. I was railroaded, plain and simple, and nothing can reclaim for me the time that was lost. Denied a lawyer of my choice and saddled with a court-appointed attorney whose greatest arguments had probably taken place in the barrooms of Baltimore, I knew the outcome before the verdict was handed down, and somewhere deep within my soul, I suspected it would span a lifetime. I have done this time without looking back. The years in prison, like dog years, have passed at a dizzying rate, each day flowing like a decade. And during this time I have done the only thing that I could do—keep moving forward.

Imprisonment is slavery and the enslavers have long been opting to pack the ships as tightly as possible. Block after block of this nation's prisons are overflowing with black and brown bodies. And after thirty years of capturing the strongest of the stock, the system now satisfies itself with our children. I am confined with young men and boys who could be my grandsons. These are youth who, prior to their imprisonment, looked to fathers and brothers and uncles for leadership only to find that, in many cases, they were already gone to the jails, the streets, or the grave. They come from mothers who have also been locked up or are frequently overburdened with basic survival issues: how to pay rent and utilities, how to feed their families, and so on. Some of them even come from middle-class backgrounds, but the common denominator is race. Most tend to be the descendants of enslaved Africans. The prison system renders the confined individual powerless, causes the separation, and in many cases dissolution, of families, and provides a labor force that in the present economy is akin to slave labor. Over time, the trauma of incarceration—being snatched away from family and community—interferes with the memory, and even though we may still recall our families and our friends, they slowly fade to little more than ghostlike figures in the shadows of our minds.

From the very moment that the cell door slammed shut, I knew it would be my responsibility to resist just like my enslaved ancestors in Virginia must have resisted. At times, that resistance would become more important than my actual innocence, for it was this determination to resist white supremacy that led to my imprisonment in the first place. Just as slavery led to the creation of the Underground Railroad, prisons have necessitated the development of a similar system comprised of relationships and routes that help the prisoner escape the inhumanity of incarceration. I have managed to hold on to my humanity for four decades now only because of the support from my family and my community, because they help me to remember that I am human.

"During the trial there were always so many people at the jail that sometimes when I went to visit I couldn't even get in." These words spoken by my mother, Ms. Eleanor Conway, thirty-eight years later are not tinged with bitterness so much as an air of regret. I am also regretful. Many people see me only through a political lens, but I am a human being, with very human relationships, yet borne of a mother who understands that I belong more to the world than her. My mother's eyes used to cloud over when she talked about the hand that I was dealt: "I never thought Eddie would still be there all these years." And I never thought I would still be here forty years later when I received word of my mother's death.

Year upon year.

The real punishment lies in the repetition of years that wind themselves around consecutive decades. They are wound so tightly that the things that comprise life even for the most ordinary of people—birthdays, graduations, weddings, births, and deaths—are lost. The milestones mark-ing one's life become legal appeals, riots and lockdowns, and transfers to other penal institutions. However mundane, however punitive, this is life in prison.

Life—what is life for the individual confined to a six-by-nine-foot cell?

Chapter One

Childhood, A Taste of America

No parent ever lays eyes on her or his newborn child and imagines that the world will snatch that baby away. Yet people of African descent have a five-hundred-year history whispering in their ears, and so mothers unconsciously cling a moment longer because they know that the world is an eager thief. There is an invisible thread that connects the generations, tying our lives together, so much so that even in the absence of kin we remain tied to their lives and experiences. For many of us this is both a beautiful and burdensome experience.

I was born April 23, 1946 at the University Hospital in Baltimore, Maryland to Eleanor and Cleophis Conway. My parents met through my Aunt Dee, my father's sister. Mom and Dee were best friends when she caught Dad's eye. They were an attractive pair, but they were as much like night and day as any couple could have been. Mom was always like a quiet stream flowing steadily through life, her calm demeanor never betraying the source of the power beneath the surface. My father, on the other hand, was the life of the party, friendly and loud. Dad pursued life to the fullest; he was a whirlwind of sorts, spinning quickly through my life. They separated sometime in 1957, simply too distinct in their own ways to unite permanently. Despite the separation, Dad remained a part of my and my sister Cookie's lives. My sister was quite close to him. I love both of my parents and I believe I have inherited traits from each. Dad was not really a womanizer, but he had a certain charm that endeared him to women, and he knew how to have fun and enjoy himself. I share that fun-loving nature and spirit, but I also recognize in myself the same quiet intensity that Mom possessed until her very last day.

My earliest memories are from 1951—the typical remembrances of a boy growing up in America at that time, like my first train set or the little red wagon that was a gift from my favorite uncle. Some recollections are less typical; one in particular still burns in my memory: I can remember being very, very thirsty one afternoon, and wandering into the house looking for something to drink. My family was out in the backyard doing summertime things, but I desperately needed to quench my thirst. Too short to reach the faucet, I spotted a glass of water sitting on the kitchen counter, and I knew if I tried real hard I could *just* reach it. I did, and I got it.

Looking back upon that incident years later, I wonder if this wasn't some sort of omen, a terrible portent warning me of things to come. The glass of clear liquid that sat on that counter calling out to me in my thirst soon had me choking and clenching my throat in agony. In my quest for relief, I had drunk nearly half a glass of bleach. My first memorable adventures in America had begun and they were caustic!

This memory returns to my mind time and again, for it seems to me an analogy for the quintessential experience of oppressed people in this country. White supremacy permeates every aspect of our lives here in the United States and the forced acceptance of it tastes much like that glass of bleach. It begins with the myth of superiority perpetuated by whites to justify the theft of resources, the conquest, genocide, and enslavement of other groups. Its consequence—an intended one—is the internalization of the myth that those of us descended from Africans are somehow inferior, and the belief that conformity to the dominant culture will make us better. A bitter and caustic lie to swallow, to be sure. Our saving grace are those pieces of the spirit that remain untouched by the lies, and that cause us to choke on this toxic lie and refuse to submit.

By 1951, the Korean War was raging in what seemed to me to be a far off corner of the world. It suddenly entered our household that year by way of the death of a relative. I can remember much discussion of the treatment of blacks in the military, and an awful lot of talk about the fact that it was us who were doing a lot of the dying in the war. In 1951, I was too young to understand that we black folks have always done a disproportionate amount of the dying, whether at the hands of one another, the white mobs, the state, or the dizzying rates of chronic illness. We die, as if black bodies, through some little known agreement with the Gods, are the sacrifice required to ensure the sustenance of humankind, and this distant relative was our family's offering. So we buried our dead soldier, but not our dreams of a better life, clinging as a family to the hope that things would get better for black folks after the war.

During those years, we lived in Cherry Hill, a neighborhood on the outskirts of Baltimore's city limits. The community was an all black public housing development that was populated with mostly low and middle income families. Though it would soon become one of the largest housing projects on the east coast, it was still under construction when I became aware of my surroundings. We were a rather large family, sometimes living under one roof. There was my grandfather and grandmother, my mother and father, as well as two aunts and an uncle, and my sister and me. My grandmother had come to Baltimore from Virginia and there was confusion about my grandfather's origins. My family had always believed that he came to America from the West Indies, though years later I learned that he was more likely mixed race, probably black and Pacific Islander, and, in fact, he had been born in Seattle. Together my grandparents had three girls: my mother and her two sisters. My father came from a fairly large family; his parents had two girls and three boys.

My sister Cookie was a year older than I, but she was always so small that it looked and felt like I was her big brother. She and I were the only grandchildren in the family at that time. There would be more children to come—my sisters Marilyn, Myra, and Peggy were the result of my mother's union with my stepfather some years later. During those early years, my mother worked outside the home as a domestic and my father was in the Navy. Dad was a veteran of World War II, and once the war ended he went to work in the Baltimore City Department of Public Works. Perhaps we were poor, but like many children of the era I didn't know it. I was well-fed and cared for by the adults around me. I sometimes still call up the memory of holidays in the house, the aroma of cakes and pies mingling with the roast turkey that my aunts cooked to perfection.

At the same time, I knew even in those early years that my situation was different than that of the white children with whom I occasionally interacted. I attended Public School #32; it was a small school in West Baltimore located on Mount Street near Riggs Avenue. When I was in the third grade, I took part in the production of a Christmas play that we were to perform at another school; turned out that this school was in a white neighborhood and the students were all white as well. It was something of a culture shock for my young mind.

One of the things that most young children learn in school is comparison and contrast. Well, I was immediately struck by the fact that their building appeared to be new and ours seemed as if it been around—and untouched—for a hundred years or so. The school itself seemed to have the latest equipment and books; we, on the other hand, had old, discarded materials handed down to us from the white schools. Our books were of the worst sort, patched bindings and fraying pages. I am certain that this experience helped to make me the man that I am, because it is especially hard to accept lies written in books that we were not able to read. The seeds of consciousness are sown early in life for children from oppressed communities, yet prior to this trip, it had never dawned on me that people lived differently in other communities. The experience left a lasting impression on many of us because we were in awe of the many things they had that we did not, like a clean, new auditorium and pool. For me, the trip was like drinking that bleach all over again and the shock was too great for me to adjust to or even justify the differences in my mind. From that point on, I lost interest in school because I knew that ours was small and dirty, and we would never have an auditorium or swimming pool.

Soon after, the "Brown vs. Board of Education" decision was handed down, and our school lives were supposed to change for the better, or so everyone thought at the time. But nothing happened, and by the next year I had failed for the first time. At the same time, I was roaming farther and farther from home with a group of neighborhood kids and my small world began to take on much larger dimensions. We would play on the railroad tracks, sometimes walking miles away from our community. Entertaining ourselves the way that poor children often do, we would make toy guns out of sticks and rubber bands and shoot at the rats that roamed the back of the huge horse stables in West Baltimore.

After the trip to the white neighborhood and school, I found that I no longer liked my own surroundings. When the city decided the next year to build a new police precinct on the same site as our house, I wasn't sorry to go. We were given ninety days to move, and after a while we settled in East Baltimore near the intersection of Preston Street and Milton Avenue. The formerly all-white community was just becoming an integrated neighborhood, and ours was only the second black family to live in the area. So all of a sudden my new friends were white, with the exception of the one black kid from the other family. It was hard for me to understand why the adults were having such a problem with us kids playing games like house, or doctor and nurse together. In particular, it was the mother of our friends next door who seemed to object the most to these domestic games, but I noticed that she didn't seem to mind us playing cowboys and Indians.

In a few short years, the neighborhood began a rapid and very obvious change as more and more whites moved out and were replaced by black families. Soon the area was a black community where the five and dime stores had suddenly turned into bars and formerly nice policemen were now mercenaries. My small world was again thrown off balance, weighted down with poverty and racism, but I still could not quite understand what was happening.

I was getting older and like many of my friends I was into riding bikes and traveling into the surrounding communities. We would get into scrapes with the white kids whose families hadn't moved further away yet. It was as if we had discovered a new land, and conquest presented the possibility of an abundant treasure trove. We would take their radios when we could, and their baseball gloves and bikes if the opportunity presented itself. There has always been this expectation of aggression where the black male is concerned, and we were simply living up to it like a child who inherits the legacy attached to a nickname, even though it may be a misnomer.

"One of these days and it won't be long, you gonna look for me and I'll be gone…"

I can still remember Ray Charles singing *I Believe* as I slow dragged in my cousin's basement with Odell, my first crush. She was a sweet redbone with a nice body that was so warm and soft that my heart started to beat fast whenever I saw her. Everything went shades of red as I planted a kiss on her lips. All these years later, I am convinced that everyone should recall their first kiss. I was still an innocent at age eleven, though bent on leaving that innocence behind and unraveling the mystery of sex. The music of my youth was rife with sexual innuendo—"Work with Me Annie" was a favorite one heard around the neighborhood, though many of us would ignore the cautionary tale in the follow up song, "Annie Had a Baby." No matter, I was on my way and there was no turning back.

Junior high school became a turning point for many of the young men in my community. Rosa Parks had started something years before down in Montgomery, Alabama. This woman's refusal to accept the status quo had helped to spark the civil rights movement and to instill a new pride in being black. What this really meant for many of us youth who were standing on the edge of adulthood was that we weren't going to take any shit from whites anymore. Youth being what it is—the emergence of a newly minted, if not mature adult—we weren't going to take any shit from anyone, or at least so we thought. At the same time, many of us young men were beginning to discover girls and the party scene. It was now very important to look hip with new clothes and material things like radios and record players, though I must admit I had more talk than game and this became apparent one afternoon when a very experienced girl pulled me under a stairwell after school and all of a sudden, sex was no longer a mystery. Needless to say, I left feeling like I was now a real man.

Our childhood excursions had evolved into real raids and forays into the nearby white neighborhoods for larger and more needed material goods. No property was safe from confiscation, neither was any person invulnerable to the shake down. Whites in cars in our community, those riding through on buses, their stores were all fair game. The older brothers in the community had set the pace and some of us younger brothers were trying to live up to their examples. Somehow we all knew, or at least believed, that our stuff had been stolen by them, and we were just getting it back using similar methods. Even if the whites had not stolen our property, the historic theft of personhood ran deep in our subconsciousness.

The varying shades of African descended people, the lack of a connection to a language, a culture, and land can only suggest like a whispered threat the depth of the true larceny. The people had so many stories about how they ended up in the holds of those slave ships. Some of them spoke of white men who waved vibrant flags that attracted them aboard the vessels. Others said that they were swept up when enemies who had once been friends raided their villages, burning huts and killing family members. No matter what the truth is, it is evident that the white man cast a wide net in which our ancestors were caught, trapped and eventually sold. The theft of personhood would resonate among the descendants for centuries to come.

Many brothers took to carrying weapons, which sometimes meant the difference between getting caught and getting away. I avoided this, but ripping off soda and milk trucks and stores during lunch breaks was a must, since these were the required activities in a constant game of "chicken" amongst peers. Soon, I had a summer job with some of the older brothers from the community who peddled goods from horse-drawn carts. In Baltimore, we refer to this phenomenon as "A-rabbing." Walking the streets with their brightly-colored wagons, the merchants would call out their goods in a sing-song refrain that has come to define, for many of us, the sound of summer in Baltimore:

"Water-*melll*-on, I got sweet red water-*melll*-on."

We went from neighborhood to neighborhood selling fruits, vegetables, and fish. I was finally making a few dollars, and in the process seeing more of the city, and I devoured the new experiences with the wide eyes of someone waking up in an entirely new environment. Through my observations, I became aware of some things that had never before entered into my consciousness. Many of the older brothers who worked on these wagons had heroin habits. It was as if this made the reality of what we saw easier for them to accept. Later in life, when I read the poem "Incident" by Countee Cullen, it would take me back to this period:

Once riding in old Baltimore
  Heart filled, head-filled with glee
I saw a Baltimorean
  Keep looking straight at me.

Now I was eight and very small
  And he was no whit bigger,
And so I smiled, but he poked out
  His tongue, and called me, "Nigger."

I saw the whole of Baltimore
  From May until December;
Of all the things that happened there
  That's all that I remember.

The difference between black and white neighborhoods, between poverty and affluence, was as stark as the difference between the white marble steps and the rotting wooden ones. The contrast between clean and dirty streets, blocks lined with trees and well-tended lawns compared to block after block of cement sidewalks lined with bars and liquor stores, said more to me than all the stories of inequality and injustice that I had heard growing up. There were few, if any, YMCAs, Lions Clubs, parks, or swimming pools in our set of run-down city blocks, while the other neighborhoods had far too many. Even this simple recognition demonstrated the difference between black and white, poverty and wealth in Baltimore during that time. I was aware of all of this, but didn't fully understand it nor would I really begin to question the cause of such disparity for some years to come.

My own community was always full of people hanging on the street corners and police cars patrolling the blocks, all of which seemed normal since there were so many fights. I soon found myself hanging on these same street corners with everyone else until all hours of the night. There wasn't really anywhere else to go or anything else to do that didn't require money, and it wasn't long before I began to run with a group of brothers who were into stealing cars and joyriding in the outlying communities. We would go to dances in our "new" cars and pick up girls to ride around with us. Drinking and partying became a way to duck the reality that nothing else was happening for us. An uncertain future and a sense of hopelessness came to define the status quo for many young black men in the urban landscape of 1960s America as industry died and jobs dwindled.

I was also was beginning to develop the "pack mentality" that many young men get when they are a part of a close-knit group, a sort of singular thinking that leads to actions on the part of a group. Once, someone among us suggested that we all serve a collective beat-down to the next individual who crossed our path. With very little thought, I participated in the beating of a black man for no reason other than the fact that we weren't willing or able to challenge ourselves to do something constructive.

In time, we began to have so much fun partying that it started to overlap with my daytime activities and hooking school soon became a regular activity. I failed again that year, and forced down yet another gulp of that bleach, fast becoming accustomed to the taste. The next year I would do better in school, but it was already too late because I was hooked on partying and girls. And, in fact, the following year I decided that school wasn't for me: I wanted to drop out and earn some money, and fool that I was, party full-time. After talking to my mother about it I soon learned that not only would she not support such a move, but I would also have to live someplace else if I dropped out. So I started looking for a real job the next day and by summer's end I was working regularly, having chosen not to return to the tenth grade.

I began the search for an apartment, which I soon found. It was 1962. I was sixteen and on my own at last and, even though I was ready and willing, I was now unable to continue partying with my friends. So eager was I to be independent that I had overlooked one simple, yet, rather important fact. I was now the sole support for myself, and I suddenly had responsibilities that would not allow me to continue partying and staying up all night. Tired, red-eyed, and hung-over from the previous night's festivities, I found that I could not get to work the next day in that shape. I was a short-order cook for an early morning lunch-wagon and after a few missed days and late arrivals, my boss made it plain that I would not be cooking much longer if it persisted.

I was finding that I had to socialize with people like myself, people with jobs and responsibilities. I began to compromise, so instead of partying all day, I began a steady pace of weekend socializing. There were four of us young men who ran around together, and between us there was a car, an apartment, and spending money. We were soon traveling up and down the east coast, and everywhere that we went there was talk of civil rights in the air. Minor incidents were going down daily between blacks and irate whites, and this was creating a serious climate change. Something was certainly happening and the mood in America was changing, but this had little, if any, real effect on us because we naively believed that the real problem was in the "south." It never occurred to us that Baltimore was also the south—that all of this country was the south when it came to oppression and racism.

The winds of this change would blow heroin into our community and it would proceed to lull the residents into a slumber that would last on into the present. Eyes glazed over, face gaunt, the heroin addict is dispossessed of spirit. She or he wanders the streets of Baltimore like a ghost from a past that still haunts our people. The addict's enslavement to the drug is an ever-present reminder of our former bondage. Baltimore would eventually become the de facto heroin capital of the United States by the early twenty-first century, and the drug became the monarch that would rule the city, even when the rest of the country was experiencing the crack-cocaine epidemic of the 1980s.

Drugs began to flow into our community as the tensions between blacks and whites started to escalate and become violent; this was no co-incidence. I managed to escape this scourge, though it would take down many from my generation. My eyes were opening to the world around me and I wanted to be fully conscious for the experience. In retrospect, I real-ize that I was fortunate enough to not be dogged by the hellhounds that nipped at the heels of my peers, especially those who had grown up in the real south, the south of beatings, lynching, and utter castration. Baltimore is south of the Mason-Dixon line and, in 2011, is probably more southern than Mississippi in 1962 in terms of segregation, but there was always the safety of numbers back then, and up until my early teens my parents had kept me away from those places where black and white intersect and sometimes conflict. My parents tried to hide the reality of second class citizenship, so they never talked about the violence of the south, beatings and lynchings. So, I was forced to figure some things out myself, and by that time we were living among whites and they were the minority.

Our group of four had now become six and we were living in a house in East Baltimore. There were three levels with an apartment on each floor. Howard and I shared the second floor apartment. My cousin, Melvin and a friend shared the first floor, while two old neighborhood friends shared the third floor. Everything conceivable to man must have happened on one floor or another during that time. The place was liter-ally open twenty-four hours a day, and there was usually a party going on most nights, with every drug imaginable available. Of course, my work schedule forced me into bed early most nights, but I was not exactly living like a monk.

Though the environment was ripe for it, there was never any real vio-lence in the house, nor did anyone ever steal a single thing from us, even though numerous people were in and out of the place every week. It was not long before hard drug traffic turned the third floor of the house into a hangout for junkies and pushers, and the situation became tense. Along with this tension came opportunity because the drugs were also drawing young women. There were occasions when we would slip up to the third floor and take advantage of some of the women who were nodding off or otherwise lost in a drug-induced semi-consciousness. This is the kind of opportunism that easily lends itself to such an environment. I am not proud of it, but I did participate in this kind of exploitation.

Things finally came to a head. Locked in my room one evening, enjoying the company of a female friend, I heard gunshots out in front of our apartment. Rushing to the window I saw my roommate Howard being shot at from a car sitting in the middle of the street. He was trying to dodge the bullets by hiding in the gutter behind a parked car. I rushed to the dresser in search of a little .22 automatic that we kept there, and, finding it, I ran back to the window and fired a few rounds, which seemed to alarm the driver, who quickly sped away. Howard and I were left wondering what had provoked this attack, so we began to ask around even though it should have been clear: the reality of the danger that accompanied drug traffic had been brought home to us. One of our buddies on the third floor was two thousand dollars in debt to a big-time drug dealer from New York.

He knew where the dude stayed when he was in Baltimore so we got some of our boys together and set out to find him. There were seven or eight of us, armed and angry. After all, our friend could have been killed on a bum tip. Some brothers fell back to cover the front and back of the house, and the rest of us went up and knocked on the door. The moment it began to open, we forced our way in, rushing through the house after leaving one old man held at gunpoint in the hallway. The dude was not there so we left a message with his uncle. We told our friend from the third floor that he had better straighten out his debts or we would force him to move out of the house.

He must have set things straight because that was the last we heard from the New York guys. Nevertheless, the general situation at the house continued to get worse, and finally one Sunday things got completely out of hand. Howard, some friends, and I went to the neighborhood movie theater around the corner to kill some time. While we were there drinking wine and getting loud, we had a beef with the rent-a-cops. Well, it turned out that they were working under the command of my future father-in-law; his daughter was three or four months pregnant with my first child. I had been seeing Kay Rogers for some time and, despite my being quite unprepared to settle down, there was a baby on the way. I found myself having to iron out the beef between our mob and the pigs since we were almost related at that point.

After leaving the movie, we returned home to find all the doors to the house had been broken open and no one was in the house. This was indeed quite strange since there was always someone in the house. Nothing was missing, but our second-floor kitchen window was broken and there was blood in the back yard. We checked with the neighbors and found out that a young woman had jumped out the kitchen window and broken several bones. The police had raided the house and locked up everyone who had been on the premises at the time. I decided at that point against staying in the house that night because everyone knew about the infamous midnight raids the police pulled in our community. Howard, on the other hand, decided to stay, and the next day when I returned from work I found out that he had been locked up. I checked with his mother, who said that he was in the Eastern District City Jail. Apparently a woman had been assaulted the night before and this had prompted the arrests. Well, she identified Howard and everyone else the police brought before her. My future father-in-law remembered all too well where Howard was during the time that the assault had taken place so he helped me get him out, but I decided that this would be the last close call for me.

Too many things were happening in that house for me to stay there any longer. I had a baby on the way and a woman I intended to marry, so I began to consider other possibilities. The relationship with Kay had moved, as those teenage romances sometimes do, too fast, and the pregnancy was the obvious result. However resolved I was to marry her and do the right thing, I was not really prepared to take on the responsibility of a family or the commitment that comes along with it. There were times when I was completely inattentive and selfish, but I was beginning to realize that the problem I was facing was not just the issue of where I was living but, rather one of where my life was going. And so, it was around this time that a few of my friends and I started talking about going into the army. The more I thought about it the better it looked and I saw it, like so many black youth still do today, as an opportunity to get out of the ghetto. Kay was getting bigger and bigger with each passing day and I would soon be a father. So on September 27, 1964, three days after the birth of my son Ronald, I decided to join up and take a new direction.

Chapter Two

Leaving Home

The process itself took only a few days, and before I knew it I was in a basic training camp in Georgia. After many weeks of long, hard training in the wet, muddy Georgia backwoods where it seemed like every day was a rainy day, the drill instructor, the exercises, and the lectures were suddenly at an end. Off we flew to advanced training in different areas. In my case, I went to Fort Sam Houston in Texas for training as a medical corpsman. There I would spend another three months that were spiced with trips to Mexico and other points west. I was beginning to see the world, be it only the western hemisphere at this point. I was rather proud of myself when I finished training as one of the top ten in our class.

I was ready to serve the nation! There was no place I would not have gone, nothing that I would not have done at that point for the good ole' US of A. And so, I was not in the least disappointed when the army decided that I would best serve the country's interest by going to Germany. New horizons were opening up before me—here I was a young black man from East Baltimore for whom even *West Baltimore* had seemed a remote spot, and suddenly I was headed to Europe. By far, this would prove to be my most profound experience up until that time, and by the time I returned home I would have a totally different view of this country and my relationship to it. But in 1964, not yet politicized, I still believed in the American dream and was prepared at all costs to do my part to uphold that fantasy.

The trip across the Atlantic by ship—more specifically, by the troop transport—was a rewarding experience for me. To behold the ocean from its center is to understand just how vast the earth is, and how small man is in comparison … a truly humbling experience. After seven days we reached land, and the German port city was a welcome sight for the many land-lovers among us. Our very first excursion was to a whorehouse where we quickly handed our money over to a woman so old and ugly that, in retrospect, it seemed like we were satisfying an odd fetish. Shortly after, I was sent out to the post where my unit was stationed. It was a medical platoon in a tank battalion, made up of twenty-two whites and two blacks, plus me. One of the blacks was a private and the other was a sergeant. Being a private myself, I paired off with the other black man of the same rank, a fellow named Goodman.

The next day, I was sent out on detail with Goodman, and every day thereafter for the next thirteen days, the two of us were sent out on one dirty detail after another. Finally, when I could take no more I spoke out in the ranks one morning as the top sergeant, a white man, made much pretense about who would go on the morning detail from our unit. Since I had been there, I had not seen a single white soldier go on one of these details. It was all too obvious to everyone in the platoon that only the black privates had been going, and since there didn't seem to be any indication that this would be changing any time soon, I yelled sarcastically, "Let Goodman and Conway go!"

This was, of course, out of order and I found myself being sent off to the company commander's office. I knew I was in big trouble being the new kid on the block in addition to getting loud with an officer in front of everyone, but I was also angry as hell. I hadn't joined the army to pick up trash, clean pots and pans, or dig holes every day, and I told the captain just that. To my great surprise, he was just as angry as I was when he learned about our treatment, and the top sergeant got an upbraiding that put an end to my details for a long time. Shortly thereafter, I became a medic and was beginning to make good on the training; most of the brothers in the battalion started coming to me if they had a problem or an injury, since they often received little or no real treatment from the white medics even though this was 1965, and almost twenty years since the armed services had been desegregated.

I would soon learn that Private Goodman had a peculiar situation that kept him in our unit. He was the victim of his own good conduct. He should have been released six months before I got to the unit, but as it turned out, Goodman had a talent that worked against him, and not even he understood it at that time. One of only two boxers in the Army in Europe in 1964, the brass wanted to keep Goodman there, and keep him fighting. So they kept charging him with minor things that would prolong his tour in the army, but not have him locked up. At first, I couldn't quite understand what was happening; everyone on the base knew who he was and how good he could fight, yet white guys would make remarks about the women who dated him within his hearing—women who were almost always white, since there were few black women in Germany at the time.

Everyone had learned by then that Goodman had a short quick temper, which was generally followed by his fists slamming into someone, so I had to wonder why these guys would pick a fight with a boxing champion. Racism aside, there had to be more to it than that because it was apparent that going up against this guy was the fastest way to an ass-whipping that any of us had ever seen. But it soon became clear to me that the army was keeping him because he was winning fights for the team. I discussed this with Goodman and he agreed to stop fighting for the army team. Within a month of his decision, Private Goodman was gone home, and I was left with the black sergeant, a man who through his actions demonstrated all that was meant when we used the term "Uncle Tom."

Fortunately, I had begun to learn my work so well that I was able to operate in a fairly independent manner. Any time something happened or someone got hurt, other soldiers on the base would send for me or for one of the two senior medics, and by that point I was doing not only my own job, but also those assigned to other members of the unit. This led to a promotion that was based in part on my ability to complete assigned tasks, and in part on the fact that I passed every test and training course they gave me. I spent a lot of time in the field with the unit under very lifelike combat conditions. The white boys did not like that kind of duty because there were no doctors or hospitals for miles around sometimes; I ate it up. Within eighteen months, I received another promotion, this time to the rank of sergeant. This would lead to contact with brothers from different units and battalions.

I was now free to roam wherever I wanted to without reporting to anyone but my unit commander, but the knowledge about the army that I began to acquire as a result of my new position shocked me. I had always been willing to listen to the problems of other brothers, and now several black GIs, who'd heard from others that I was a stand-up type of sergeant, started coming to me with all types of reports. They informed me about Klan meetings in their billets at night, unfair racial promotion policies, and, like my own earlier experience, many of them reported that dirty duty details always went to black GIs. Unfortunately, many of these things were beyond my ability to resolve, but just seeing a peer, a black man, as a sergeant gave them hope. I was gradually awakening to the fact that the US army was no place for a brother.

The day that everything changed ... well, it started off just like every other one. Getting out of bed was never very easy for me, and this particular morning was no exception. Any eagerness to leave the comfort of my bunk was being hindered greatly by the aftereffects of my partying the night before. I had had a few drinks too many; drinking was becoming a regular part of army life for me. My assistant brought me breakfast and a newspaper, and the food and coffee was helping to get me ready for the day. The troops had been up and out for at least two hours. Rank having its privilege, I didn't have to show up until I wanted to. I let my assistants alternate their duties weekly because more work got done that way, and this seemed more effective than me hovering around.

It was July 1967. As I sat there eating, my eyes scanned the morning newspaper. What I saw there staring back at me made me forget my hangover completely. There on the page was a photograph of an American soldier aiming a .50 caliber machine gun at a group of unarmed black women gathered on a street corner in Newark, New Jersey, as they stood with their arms raised and fists clenched in protest. The women were obviously discontented and angry as hell with the soldier who was perched safely atop an armored personal carrier, his finger planted firmly on the trigger of one of the Army's most sophisticated weapon systems—right in the heart of a black community.

I stared at the picture uncomprehendingly, unable to process what I was seeing; when I finally managed to tear my eyes away from the horror unfolding in front of me, I could only stare into my open locker at the heavily starched olive-green uniforms hanging there. On the sleeves of each one were the symbols of my dedication, three neatly sewn yellow stripes. The rays of the morning light were glinting off of the highly polished boots that stood below the uniforms, but the sunlight wasn't strong enough to illuminate the reality of what was happening in the world, nor did it shed any light on the unrealistic role I had been playing in it all. I say unrealistic because there has always been this saying among black folks that a black man doesn't belong in uniform. This speaks to the fact that we could serve in the army, in defense of this country, but be denied the most basic human rights, be lynched, and be treated as second-class citizens. Yet, we still put on the uniform in hopes that it will change the conditions that we live in. Though my soul was beginning to pull away from that cloth, here I was, a black soldier in Germany doing his part to uphold democracy and the great *American* principles of justice for all, freedom from oppression, and so on. I was defending the American way of life—the right of all men to be free. Wasn't I?

I just could not fathom what a white soldier, or any soldier for that matter, would be doing on *any* corner in our country with a weapon pointed at a group of unarmed women; *American* women. I couldn't imagine why he was there, or what thoughts were going through his head as he held the possibility of life or death over dozens of black women. *American women.* I certainly could not conceive how anyone could have ordered such a show of force, let alone why anyone would follow such an order. The one thing I did know, however, was this: if that soldier would have sneezed, more than half of those fragile black bodies would have been dead. The faces in the photo were not unlike the faces of the family and friends I had left behind—in fact, I had a growing sense of awareness that my family, my friends, or even my mother could have just as easily been standing on the very same corner in Baltimore facing the same guns. I grabbed my robe and the newspaper and walked out into the hall, in search of answers to the scores of questions that flooded my mind.

There I stood in the middle of the hall, half-dressed, stopping anyone I could, shoving the newspaper in their face, and demanding to know what they thought of this newest development in what I was coming to understand was the modern face of American racism. To my great dismay, the responses I received were apathetic at best. My last hope was to find my friends; surely they would be able to help me to understand what the hell was going on and, more importantly, what we should be doing about it. It was about 9AM when I located them on the parade grounds. I must have looked wild, running up to them in the middle of the grounds dressed in my bathrobe, unshaven and with my hair obviously uncombed; this was simply something one did not do in the midst of a military encampment.

At the time, though, I couldn't have cared less what the Army considered normal. As far as I was concerned, the image in that newspaper demonstrated that the whole Army itself, and the government as well, was behaving abnormally. I didn't yet understand that this show of force was actually typical of the government's response to nonconformity on the part of people of color. So I naively posed my questions, but no answers were to be found among my friends. There was very little knowledge to be had among most of the black soldiers stationed in Europe. These rebellions seemed like a new phenomena, and no one I spoke with was certain what was causing them. Most of my peers were just as confused as I was, if not quite as curious. I left there with a feeling of dejection and made my way back to the confines of my quarters. Thinking back on the racism I had experienced in my life, I came to realize that I had always viewed these isolated incidents of resistance and repression as just that: isolated incidents, individual acts that were the result of a specific instance of misguided bigotry. But now I was beginning to see that this was a much larger problem, and it was one that was government-sanctioned.

We had all been kids when we signed up for the army: my two friends, Knowles and Newkirk, my future brother-in-law, Boot, and myself. Having enlisted together we had planned to stay together. Yet Uncle Sam had a different plan, and I was sent to Germany, while our two buddies stayed in the States. Unfortunately, my brother-in-law ended up in Vietnam and within eleven months of his arrival, his lifeless body lay face down in the middle of a cow pasture where his squad had been ambushed. It took three months for me to receive word of his death. He was one of my closest friends and his death hit me hard. The loss of someone so young and vibrant always strikes at the heart. As youth, we were so unprepared for death because we thought we would live forever. None of us could see the deathly shadow that hung so heavily over our generation, yet it was there: Vietnam. Angry and unable to articulate my feelings of loss and grief, I made plans to go. I needed to lash out at someone. This is the dilemma of the man of African descent in this country: oppression quite naturally creates anger and all too often that emotion is folded up in the confusion of being "American," and then it is directed not at the oppressor, but at the first available target, who quite often looks like us.

I signed up for combat duty, and having less than a year left to serve, found out that I would have to re-enlist for two more years in order to receive the training and serve a full tour. All I wanted was to go to Vietnam and sit behind a .50 caliber machine gun and kill as many Vietnamese as possible to avenge this death that I felt so much guilt about. Boot had wanted to be like me so much that he had given little thought to joining the army; he had been following my lead. And now, here I was contemplating the best way to get the training and promotion I would need to have some control over my situation once I was in Vietnam fighting to avenge Boot's death.

Boot's death had occurred some months before this photo found its way into my barracks, but suddenly I was confronted with a new reality and I no longer wanted to go to Vietnam and kill people who had not done me any harm. The visions of stars and stripes had faded and I no longer felt that sense of loyalty to the old red, white, and blue. For me, it was time to consider the red blood that was being spilled by black bodies. All the people who had fought—my relative, Boot, and now these women whose defiance made them targets—they all represented the various degrees of sacrifice that we, the descendants of enslaved Africans, had made. So I wondered how the United States Army could be in Vietnam under the premise of protecting citizens' rights there, yet standing ready to murder unarmed black women in Newark.

I posed a question to myself: what was the difference between those black women standing on that corner in America and the brown women standing at the edge of their villages in Vietnam? There was less difference and more in common. My uncle and Boot had died for the same government that now turned their crosshairs on both groups of women. It was then that I came to the realization that I was in the wrong army. I would never wear that American uniform again as I had worn it all this time, with pride. I put on some civilian clothes and went to ask for emergency administrative leave.

The company commander approved my leave and I caught the first train heading away from Germany. I had no idea where I was headed; I only knew that I needed to get away from the insanity of the world around me. I was angry and I didn't really know why. Memories of Baltimore and those bike rides through the affluent white neighborhoods flooded my mind, and nudged at my sleeping anger. My discontent stretched out before me, uncurling like a tiger that had fallen asleep on an empty stomach. The roar was deafening, and no matter how hard I tried, I couldn't get past the feeling that I was living in a parallel universe that left me out of pace with the everyday world around me.

My travels eventually took me to Copenhagen in Denmark, which seemed like the best place for me to pull myself together before I lost all that I had worked for during the past few years; I needed to tread carefully, even though I found myself questioning what the hell I had been working for anyway. The army had proved to be as deceptive as that glass of bleach all those years ago, only now I was unable to consume the lies. I took to burying my thoughts in drink and women, spending most of my time haunting the bars and night clubs of the city. At that particular moment, Copenhagen was a haven for young black men—Africans who had left the continent, African Americans who were dodging the draft so that they might avoid the war in Vietnam, and others like me, in self-imposed exile. Denmark offered a racial openness that many of us from the U.S. had never known.

Staying up all night and sleeping all day was my way of trying to forget what was happening in the world and the contradictions that I was faced with. It seemed as if all of the sergeants in the Army with over five years in were heavy drinkers; I wondered if they too weren't ducking reality. These all-nighters helped to obstruct the truth, and it worked until the night I went to a play called *Patrick X*. It was based on the life and death of Malcolm X, and it was traveling throughout Europe during 1966 and '67. Few people in Europe were even aware of who Malcolm X was or why he had been assassinated, myself included. Sitting in the audience, I slowly began to sense the importance of the role he had played in black people's struggle in America, and to realize just how much this role had to do with his untimely demise. I left the playhouse haunted by Malcolm's legacy and wondering why a play was being shown in Europe about this black man who had been assassinated only a year or so before.

That night, I decided to investigate Malcolm X's life and his writings. I started off reading the little pamphlets and articles that were being sold at the play; these were written by and about him. Then at some point I read *The Autobiography of Malcolm X* by Alex Haley, and gradually I ran across more material about Malcolm X while rummaging through bookstores in Copenhagen. This was the first time that I had ever looked at black writers, or even read about the American experience as seen through the eyes of black people. This would lead me to read other works by both black and white writers on subjects like politics, economics, oppression, and liberation struggles. It was only after reading a number of books and other materials that I realized that not only was there a race problem, but also a class struggle, and that both were related, and both were worldwide. Yet, even at this point I still believed in the American dream, still believed that things could be corrected, as a matter of fact I never considered that they wouldn't, because I really believed that along with the blacks who were struggling, there had to be enough good whites who wanted to see change. Right?

During my search for myself I met a sister from Africa and started meeting some brothers from the small African community in Denmark. The first thing I discovered was that most of these Africans looked down on American blacks as being subservient at worst, and worthless at best. As far as they could see, we served the enemy, but I was so angry with the American set that I found acceptance among them because I was different. Soon, my circle of friends consisted of several of these African brothers and some black GI's who had gone AWOL, as well as a few black draft dodgers who had begun to show up in the wake of the war in Vietnam. We hung out in a particular section of the city where there were several bars and nightclubs, one of which was a spot called, and this is no joke, the Dew Drop Inn; every town must have one.

One evening my African lady and I were dining there, and there was a small group of Africans enjoying themselves at one of the nearby tables and the atmosphere was very pleasant. Just as the waiter was serving us our meal, a white American couple came in and sat at the table next to us. He was a sergeant and seated next to him was a rather homely woman who had to be his wife. The noise from the table where the Africans sat grew to a minor roar and this seemed to upset the American and his wife. He bullishly requested that they hold the noise down, and of course the Africans ignored him until his repeated requests became a nuisance. Then they replied by telling him to mind his own business. This, of course, brought the sergeant to his feet and the Africans responded in kind. All were ready to fight and, since I was right there in the middle with my lady, I stood up to attempt to straighten the situation out. The American made eye contact with me, and perhaps because I was standing, assumed that I was a fellow American soldier who was on his side. Based on this assumption he invited the others outside though I still intended to resolve the conflict.

Once outside, the sergeant proceeded to attack the Africans. I was pissed off because of the manner in which he had dealt with the brothers and the assumption that I was going to help him because we were both Americans. It wasn't supposed to matter who or why we were fighting; the only thing that mattered was that both he and I were from America. After all whose side was I supposed to be on? With that in mind I jumped into the fight and helped ... the Africans. Shortly thereafter I had to return to my unit, so I donned the uniform one more time, caught a plane to the States and signed out of the Army for good.

Chapter Three

Home Is Where the Hatred Is

I had been away from America for three years; it was now 1967 and my first impression was that everything in Baltimore had changed. There were new buildings on new streets, new cars, and new gadgets. There were empty lots where buildings used to be. Everything was much more advanced, including my own perspective. I had left for Germany as a teenager, a child; but the shift in values I had experienced during my tour of duty, the contradictions I had seen during my service to this country, and those I had experienced within myself *because* of my service to my country, now forced me to see America through the eyes of a man, a black man, to be precise. For the first time, I took a close look at the American way of life—and what I saw began to make me think that the *American* way of life posed a real threat to the survival of black people, and of poor people everywhere.

While I was stationed in Europe, we constantly referred to the United States as "the world." We would sit around and share plans for what we intended to do when we got back to "the world." In our ignorance, we thought that everywhere else was backwards and uncivilized, with their antiquated buildings, farms, outhouses, and funny little cars. Their technology seemed inferior to our own, despite being, in all actuality, more advanced in some areas. Things made in America always seemed better to us than others, though we never had any real proof to back this observation up. This thinking extended to people, and we behaved arrogantly; this is the mindset that many US citizens still carry to many parts of the *real* world.

So, it was with eyes opened wide to that world that I returned to Baltimore, and moved in with my mother, stepfather, and three younger sisters, all of us living together in a house on Federal Street, near Greenmount Avenue, in what was and still is a very impoverished neighborhood. This area of Baltimore is near the cemetery where the remains of Johns Hopkins and John Wilkes Booth are interred, and in those days at least, the dead were perhaps the only whites in the immediate neighborhood. Federal Street runs east to west and ends at the front wall of this cemetery, picking up on the other side. The poverty and despair found there create a literal dead end for a good number of the community's residents, many of whom never get back up once they bump into that wall.

My son's mother, Kay Rogers, moved into this house with us, though we moved into our own apartment on 25th Street once we married later that year. Those days were to be the best ones that I would spend with Ronald, who was by then three years old. I was eager to share my life lessons with him, but I found myself continually playing catch-up, because I had left the States immediately after his birth and had seen him only once until I was discharged. I had left Baltimore for Europe determined to explore a new world and spent my leave exploring the Continent instead of traveling home to visit my family—and as a result, had already missed many of Ronald's formative experiences. Yet the knowledge that my son would have to grow up in the world that surrounded me helped to fuel my desire to build a better black community, and it was this desire that would ultimately push me in a more radical direction. In retrospect, I realize that I lacked the balance necessary to create a strong family unit, but at the time, I honestly thought that everything I did was ultimately for the benefit of my son. It is, perhaps, ironic that so much of my work was dedicated to creating a better community, a better world for my son—I could never have predicted the complexities that would result from my being imprisoned most of his life. Neither did I understand all of what it took to be a father and husband. My marriage to Kay lasted only about a year and a half, although we remained friends, and throughout the years we continued to collaborate on raising Ronald.

After a few months back in the States, I took a second look around me: I had begun to recognize the same old buildings, the same shanties and inferior living conditions that had plagued the regions of the world I had just been fighting to "liberate." Once I left the city's downtown area, it was like being in a third-world country. Rusting cars lined the alleys, and uncollected garbage was just around the corner and out of sight from the main thoroughfares in most working-class and poor communities. Old people huddled in groups and stayed close to home for protection. The American technology we had bragged about throughout the war was concentrated in certain small areas for the benefit of a small group of people. Drugs flowed freely, and would soon ensnare many of the residents in this *other* Baltimore.

About three months after my return to the US, I got a job at a prominent Baltimore university hospital as an operating room technician. As a glorified orderly, it was my job to rotate from room to room setting up the major pieces of machinery necessary for the operation scheduled in each. I was rather hopeful at this time about the possibility of elevating my status in the field by attending medical school. I intended to use my GI-Bill benefits to cover most of the cost, while I continued working in the hospital to gain the practical experience I was sure to need in the future.

Within a matter of months, though, I got a general picture of the operating room traffic, and it wasn't a pleasant one. The number of black males who were coming in with gunshot wounds resulting from police confrontations was very high and the treatment they received was not all that good. All gunshot victims came first to the emergency room and were then rushed into surgery should the case require it. One situation in particular caught my eye: a young black victim, who seemed to be about 5'11" and maybe 190 pounds, had been admitted to the emergency room; he had a bullet lodged in his lower calf muscle. There was some bleeding, but the wound did not seem to be severe.

In fact, the doctors who were present behaved very nonchalantly, as if they did not care. Their attitude toward the patient bordered on hostile, though this could have been a result of the fact that a police officer was present in the operating room talking and joking with them. Certainly the seriousness and care that one would expect in such a situation did not prevail. The nurses were just as unconcerned and even found time to joke about the young man's dirty feet. Although I had observed hundreds of operations by this time, I had never witnessed such a display of absolute disregard among doctors and nurses. When the bullet was removed and the operation was over the patient was wheeled away to the intensive care unit, where I checked to see how he was doing before I finished my shift.

His condition was stable, but he was still unconscious. When I returned the next morning, I learned that the young man had died sometime during the night, supposedly from heart failure.

This didn't feel right to me; but he was dead and there was nothing I could do about it. I stored the incident away in the back of my mind, but it swam back to the front when I started hearing rumors as time went on about poor people being used as unwitting organ donors for wealthier patients. Older black workers at the hospital and people in the community had seen poor families signing over the bodies of their loved ones to the hospital "in case of death," in return for free medical treatment that frequently did result in the death of the patient on the operation table. I knew that some of these stories were as old as the hospital itself and I tried to separate fact from fiction; but this particular facility had, in those days, some of the most racist and insane medical personnel I had seen after four years of working in hospitals. I began watching the attitudes and behavior of the doctors and nurses closely, determined to protect the lives and the rights of the patients who came through.

One day I had to prepare the operation room for a mastectomy. A middle aged black woman had been diagnosed with cancer and needed to have both of her breasts removed. This was a fairly standard 3-hour procedure and it had been scheduled from noon to 3PM. As the nurses and I prepared the main operating area for the surgery, the doctor came into the scrub room to prepare himself. I noticed that he had on a golfing outfit, but thought nothing of it since doctors often wear street clothes up to the operating room floors. I overheard him tell an assistant that he had a game at 1PM, and wondered about that. I knew that it was possible to have another doctor come in and finish the operation by closing up the cuts and doing the post-op work, but it would be impossible for him to do the entire operation by himself and still get to his golf game on time. The surgeon began his work, nonetheless, and after forty-five minutes there was real concern in the room.

He was using an electric scalpel, a highly sophisticated instrument that can only be used at a very particular speed, so as to make precise cuts while burning blood vessels closed without frying them. Too swift of a movement, and a cut may start to bleed, leaving only hand-applied pressure to stop it. Too slow of a movement and the scalpel may fry closed the veins and capillaries. Dr. Golf was cutting at such a rapid pace that the patient was bleeding tremendously and her blood was everywhere. It was obvious to everyone present that the doctor was butchering this woman. His assistant had begun to show agitation and the nurses were visibly upset, but the doctor paid them no regard. There is a very real hierarchy in the operating room, and no one is willing to step out of line, even in a situation like the one I had found myself in. The operation was over by 1:30. We transferred the patient to the intensive care unit and ten minutes later she was dead.

I was surely angry about this and it might have passed as just another wound in my memory bank—another swig of that bleach—stored away with the rest, but as chance would have it, I passed the dead woman's daughter and her husband on my way to another part of the hospital, and overheard the doctor telling them the sad news, with assurances that he had done all he could to save her. But the straw that broke the camel's back ... well, the whole time, he had his golf gloves and cap behind his back. That was enough for me. My very own grandmother had died after receiving questionable treatment at this same hospital, as was so often the case with poor blacks. The treatment often came too late because their money was short, and when they did finally seek treatment, the results were frequently negligible when they happened to run in with a doctor whose racist perceptions affected the value he placed on black lives. I went up to the grieving family, and I told them that this man had killed their wife and mother with a rushed job so that he could go and play a game of golf. He tried to put me back in my place at first, and failing that, he tried to pretend that the operation was just too complex for us to understand.

I just couldn't take any more and I punched him in the mouth. I couldn't allow this butcher to tell those lies to the family of the woman he had just butchered. After all, this was not Nazi Germany, right? He was not going to enjoy his game of golf that day. "Killer!" I yelled as other hospital personnel pulled me away. I knew once again that I was in trouble, but I didn't care. I told the family that I would call the local newspapers and report the incident; this man was a murderer and we should do something about it. The other employees dragged me away. I don't know what the poor family was thinking about all of this. I was out of order, yet again, and it wasn't long before the supervisor sent for me.

I wasn't taking no for an answer. I didn't want to hear any of things they said that implied I didn't know what was really going on in the operating room that day, or believe their claims that only the doctor was knowledgeable enough to understand what might cause a patient to die. I knew what I had heard and, more importantly, I knew what I had seen. This man was guilty as hell, and I continued to demand that he be charged with murder by the hospital. The supervisor continued to tell me that I was just a layman, that he was a doctor, and so, really, my word didn't mean a damn. I was the one who had hit a doctor and slandered him in front of witnesses. Eventually, we got down to the real deal. They would transfer me to another hospital and see that I did not have any problem getting into medical school. They offered to help me by providing any kind of assistance I might need, as long as I didn't make waves for the hospital. It sounded like a good deal, but I just couldn't go for it. I had watched too many dirty deals go down, with black people being on the receiving end one time too many. I wanted to make waves. We had to put a stop to this stuff because it just wasn't right. I left and went back to the people who had worked that operation with me, but I was in for another shock: I hadn't realized it at the time, but I was the only black person in that operating room, except for the woman on the table.

The only other person of color who had been present—and I am talking about at least ten people—turned out to be a Korean nurse. So after I talked to everyone else, and received no support, I went to her and pulled her aside. I asked her why she didn't seem upset, and why she had let this happen. She told me that this type of thing goes on all the time and that there was nothing she or anyone else could do about it. In short, the doctors were going to stick together, cover up for each other. She did not want to get involved, and she told me I should get a grip on myself. Obviously, I was out of step with what was going on. When I realized that I was not going to get any help from the other staff members, I decided that the best thing to do was find a black doctor. I thought that if I found a black doctor and brought this case to his attention he would at least check into it. Once that happened, I knew the reports and records would reflect facts that were impossible to deny: you just cannot do a three-hour operation in one hour. He would know that this was a case of negligence and that a murder had been committed and would speak out. And, in my naievete, I assumed that the hospital would act quickly then, and this quack would go to jail. Of course, I was wrong.

There I was roaming up and down the hallways of the hospital looking for a black doctor. I found hundreds of doctors before I could find one black. The first one I found was working in pathology and he refused to be bothered with what I was saying and told me right off that ninety percent of the deaths at Hopkins were blacks and that the hospital was doing the best it could. So, I went and found the second doctor who was working in the blood lab as a technician. When I opened the door and walked in I knew it was all over for this whole thing. There he was carrying a tray filled with a coffee pitcher and cups, donuts, sugar, and cream and serving all the lab techs and doctors in the room; everyone in there was white except him. He was making inquiries: "Two sugars or three, chocolate or plain?" That picture told me the whole story, but I had to try. He just could not get involved because he was paying back his school loans and had to steer clear of conflicts.

I even tried to call the newspapers in the hopes that someone would follow up on the situation, but it was apparent that they thought it was just another baseless rumor. After the racism in the Army, racism in the medical community was hard to swallow. The fact that black people were being killed in the very places they were going for help was a situation that I didn't like, but the truth seemed to be that nobody who had any real power gave a fuck about what was happening. I had to find another job because I had gone way out on a limb on this one, and I was sure that I couldn't continue to work around people who were butchering black patients or silently watching others doing it. They really didn't care, so I decided to contact some of the local civil rights organizations and see if this issue could be taken to the human rights commissions or somebody. We even discussed calling Governor Agnew.

This attempt at bringing justice to what I deemed an unjust situation would prove to be a study in slow motion, and while it was going nowhere I still needed to find a job. At the time, there was an organized effort to integrate both the fire and police departments at the Sparrows Point plant of Bethlehem Steel. Once I got into the employment office they immediately sent me over to the area for pipe fitters and general labor. I informed them that this was not the type of work that I was looking for, and asked what other openings they might have. When I asked about the firefighters positions they gave me the old line "you have to be qualified," and suggested that I take another job. Once it was understood that I was not changing my mind about the job I was sent off to take a series of tests.

I passed all of the tests and was informed that I had to pass the training before I could actually have the job. I went to the training course, passed, and finally got the job—and found myself right back in the middle of another racial battle.

The difference, of course, was that this time I had chosen to be right where I was, and I became very combative, to say the least. There were 101 firefighters at Sparrows Point, of which 95 were white and six were black. As a rule, the six of us would get most of the isolated duty at the outpost or fire patrols of the shipyard. During the times I got daytime duty at the main firehouse station, we sat around like any other fire department, playing cards and bullshitting, or watching TV waiting for the bell to ring, while hoping that it wouldn't. I would witness a number of things while I was there, like the constant talk about arming the firefighters against the "animals" (meaning blacks and hippies), and selling and trading guns. There was also hate literature being distributed and secret meetings by what looked like a Klan group in the department. Of course, by this time I was angry as hell and every chance I got I jumped into their gatherings and discussions, taking them to task every time I heard a racist assumption.

They would say things like, "Why are all those black women on welfare while all the men are riding around in Caddys?" They wondered why their tax money should go to support all these freeloaders, as if they were the only ones paying taxes. I just kept pointing out the fact that twice as many whites were on welfare as blacks, and that most of the money for welfare went to their friends and family in the form of social service jobs and grants for training that we never got. Of course, they weren't trying to listen to an angry nigger with facts, and it wasn't long before I was getting all my duty at the outpost and on midnight ship patrol.

I was working for the fire department in April 1968 when Dr. Martin Luther King, Jr. was assassinated. I had felt for some time that King's importance for black people had begun to wane; his commitment to nonviolence in the face of such extreme force seemed to have lost its resonance in our community. Black people were tired, angry, and frustrated. The time had come for us to do more than just sing in the streets and march on capitals—not that we necessarily knew what else to do at the time, but it was certainly clear that we needed to change the strategy. The fact that Malcolm X and Martin Luther King had been assassinated within three years of each other was too much for many blacks, and the result came in the form of the riots that raged across the nation.

It was around this time that members of the Black Panther Party became visible in Baltimore city. Four members of the party from New York got locked up for allegedly burning down parts of a shopping center in Cherry Hill, the Baltimore neighborhood where I had lived as a young child, because the center refused to close in honor of Dr. King's death. There were armed confrontations between black and white communities that bordered each other. There were also some confrontations in the heart of black communities when white store owners drew weapons on crowds of blacks to protect their property. After seeing guns in the hands of everyone else in almost all the communities surrounding their own, the mood among blacks soon changed.

Black people in general, but especially young blacks, started arming themselves. The police response to the riots—and the use of the National Guard—played a key role in this change. During the riots there were no less than six different types of police patrolling the community. These forces operated independently of one another, each demonstrating different behavior and attitudes toward the community's population. At any given time, the Baltimore City Police, Baltimore County Police, Maryland State Troopers, FBI, the United States Army, and the National Guard, as well as officers from the Department of Natural Resources, might be actively patrolling in Baltimore. Since I had a firefighters' uniform (i.e. boots, helmet, and the coat), I was able to move around fairly easily, but always under the pretext of heading to work because, with the amount of fires burning, every firefighter in the state was needed. In most cases, my credential and uniform covered me, but there still were some risky times just being a black man on the streets.

The patrols were all-white *and* armed, yet this was really nothing new, for Baltimore *is* the south, and armed white racists at that time were merely a part of the southern landscape. However, to experience such an encounter in the midst of a race riot is akin to finding a fuel tank in a burning house: it was explosive, to say the least, and I suffered a lot of abuse during the riots.

When it all ended, a lot of black folks got together to talk about organizing to deal with these problems on another level. A number of small groups had sprung up and some of them went public while others remained underground. By this point, I had also had enough, and felt that it was time to start dealing with the oppression of black people. I began working with a group of brothers who also felt the need for change. We stayed together for a few months talking and sharing information about national black groups that were forming and growing. The Blackman's Liberation Army was spreading out of Washington D.C. and into Baltimore and Virginia; this organization should not be confused with the Black Liberation Army. The Blackman's Liberation Army was a short-lived entity that was a direct result of the 1968 riots. SNCC (Student Non-Violent Coordinating Committee) had become more militant, and even CORE (Congress of Racial Equality) had changed its image and assumed a more militant position. The Black Panther Party had grown, with chapters from California to New York. At the same time, a regional network of Black Nationalist groups were beginning to operate together, and so it was not hard to do research on the new groups and developments, especially since most of these groups put out weekly literature. Insurrection was in the air.

Resistance is a natural response to oppression, and the story of people of African descent in the western hemisphere is one of rebellion and broken shackles. Women and men marching on; these ragtag armies of black, brown, and yellow soldiers armed with farm tools, the occasional musket, and a plan to kill the slave master. Rising up out of their bondage, the rebels intended to be free in this world, or the next. Get free, or die trying. Charles Deslondes. Makandal. Nat Turner. These names would produce a fear so strong in the whites that the thought of an armed and angry black man would echo that fear for generations to come. The race struggles of the late 1960s called to mind this same fear and anger.

Eventually, our small group split three ways; one segment wanted to go with the nationalist network, another wanted to continue working as a small group, and the third wanted to join the Panthers. Obviously, I was in the latter; I had come to believe that something very serious was happening to black people, and it was neither a local phenomenon nor was it totally about racial discrimination. We couldn't continue to address the plight of black people through lawsuits and Supreme Court rulings, as the civil rights movement had done. black people in the north had been asserting our right to vote, but we were still treated as second-class citizens. It wasn't just an issue of going to the polls. The struggle then as now was about human rights. I believed that the problem was larger than it appeared and that the Black Panther Party had the best program for addressing it. Those of us who felt like the BPP was the answer actively searched out the local Panthers and joined up with them only to find that the Baltimore Panthers were very few, and being a relatively new chapter, unorganized. It would become my mission for the next several years to build and develop the Baltimore branch.

The Black Panther Party for Self-Defense, founded in Oakland, California in October 1966, was recognized by many from its inception as an armed opposition organization against the US government. The organization's philosophy declared racism, capitalism, and the US government enemies of the African American community. A nationalistic and class-based ideology caused law enforcement agencies to label the organization a nationalist hate group with a communist paradigm early in its development. The Black Panther Party gained rapid recognition in the San Francisco Bay Area because of its armed police patrols on the one hand, and its radical anti-imperialist ideology on the other. Fundraising activities such as selling Chinese Chairman Mao's *Little Red Book* at area universities and colleges spread the group's message to white radicals. The Panthers soon established a newspaper that helped to explain the organization's policies and positions to a wider audience. Local chapters could be organized in any African American community with training and approval from the national headquarters. All chapters reported to the National Central Committee, and followed their instructions.

In Baltimore, we quickly found that we had to keep shifting the office location from place to place because we lacked funds and had very little support. But there was always a little office somewhere that that we could meet in, and so we carried on, although the local chapter initially seemed more like a social group than a political organization, and I sometimes thought that they were misinterpreting the meaning of the word "party." The office was initially located on Valley Street in West Baltimore in the house of one of the founding members, Warren Hart, a man who would later be exposed as an agent operating for the National Security Agency. Next the office moved to Eden Street in East Baltimore, and finally to the 1200 block of Gay Street, also in East Baltimore. Sometime after my arrest, the office would once again relocate.

I had already begun to learn that heart alone did not a revolutionary make. Neither the logistical instability nor the lack of serious commitment to the revolution on the part of some members would deter me though, because I was already becoming deeply involved in the politics of the party. Any discouragement that I felt early on was quickly turned around as many serious people began to join our ranks. This brought on the first major actions that we would take as a party to support the political struggles going on in Baltimore's black community around control of the Deaprtment of Education department. Soon, we were demonstrating at Memorial Stadium against Nixon's destructive domestic and foreign policies because both were having an impact on our communities. The simple fact of sisters and brothers coming together on a regular basis to work for the community and expand their knowledge brought a new level of consciousness to the group.

It was during this time that we began to see that there was a movement afoot to dismantle the progress of the BPP. Huey P. Newton, founder and National Leader of the BPP, had been locked up in Oakland, California for a police shooting. Co-founder Bobby Seale was arrested when he went to the 1968 Democratic Convention in Chicago. Then Eldridge Cleaver went into exile after a shooting that resulted in the murder of Little Bobby Hutton by the Oakland California Police Department. It was soon very clear that we were being attacked on every front as the general climate in America became overtly hostile toward the Panthers and other groups dedicated to self-determination. The directive from Hoover was clear: search and destroy.

Chapter Four

Work Is Struggle

It was of vital importance to our struggle that all party members were well-informed, so everyone was required to attend political education classes twice a week in order to remain in good standing. We took these classes very seriously because there were consequences attached to slacking: running a mile was the standard punishment, yet the bigger consequence was a lack of knowledge. During the initial formation of the party it became clear that we had to look to the struggles of other peoples, especially those in the so-called "third world" for some of the solutions to our problems. The political education classes were held at night in the offices after most members returned from their daily assignments and had their supper.

I was so thoroughly convinced that the BPP was the best instrument for change available to black folks that I even asked my mother to join. She once told a friend of mine that, while she had family obligations that would not permit her to join us, she never objected to what I was doing and in fact, many of the older people she knew were glad that the Panthers were active in the community. Widespread community support was of critical importance to the Panthers, and we always took great care to take heed of the voices of the community—something that I have continued to abide by in my organizing work in prison.

But, back to the past: at the time, many party members lived on the floors above the offices on Gay Street, which had bedrooms upstairs and a few cots downstairs. A decent number of members could sleep over on any given night that they wanted to, and many did because of the late hours we kept. On the nights that we held the political education classes, everyone would gather in the classroom while the assigned lieutenant would start the class off with a brief rundown on something that was in our newspaper, *The Panther*, and we would discuss the chosen article, which was usually about new policies or some major event that affected the BPP or black communities. These were also the things that we would discuss with the people we came into contact with in the neighborhoods.

Most of our members were young people looking to be a part of something that would change the status quo in this country. These youth had often seen their parents struggle economically while also contending with Jim Crow laws and practices. Many of the young women in the party had also come from a tradition where women assumed so-called "non-traditional" roles; women of African descent always have. I found it important to treat these women as comrades. During the early part of my involvement with the Panthers, Kay and I were still together and she participated in some of our party activities, so it was also important to me to show every woman the respect that they were due. However, there were the usual complications that occur when passions flare both politically and otherwise. On one occasion, a young woman I had come to know and work with attempted suicide. She had been pursuing me relentlessly and when I did not respond she shot herself. Fortunately it was only a flesh wound in the leg, but she was expelled from the party.

The *Little Red Book*, otherwise known as "Quotations from Chairman Mao Tse Tung," was the foundation for most of our classes. Although we used other textbooks, the *Little Red Book* remained the main text throughout the party's history and during this time it became the most popular revolutionary book in America. I don't know if that was because we were using it or if it was being used because of that, but it was easy to obtain and written so simply that it was easy for most people to understand. It became the lifeblood of the BPP's political training program. All conflicts or confrontations would send the disagreeing parties dashing off to find their copy of the *Little Red Book* to resolve the debate. The *Little Red Book* was the final word on any subject; not even party directives or rules survived if they were in real disagreement with the *Little Red Book*.

We would sometimes spend hours during a class examining a key chapter of the book, with each passage read aloud and discussed by the whole class until there was a general agreement that everyone understood the subject matter. We were young and eager to advance our thinking, and our strong desire for learning was reflected by the fact that we spent hours each night reading and discussing this or that subject from the *Little Red Book*.

Our thirst for knowledge was a result of our wish to see a better socio-economic arrangement for our people and communities. We simply needed the truth, having been handed lies all of our lives. As we gained knowledge, some of us worked to establish offices in other areas of the region like South Baltimore and Annapolis and got involved in these communities' political issues.

In Baltimore, the chapter had begun organizing around some problems at Frederick Douglass High School, and a public rally we helped to put together in support of the community's concerns would soon result in two carloads of Panthers being arrested on trumped up charges. The falsified charges were later dropped, but this would set the tone for our future dealings with Baltimore city officials, especially the police department. It was the start of what would soon become weekly police harassment of the Baltimore Black Panther Party. Our members were being arrested in ever-increasing numbers for very minor things, and this soon escalated from situations like traffic stops and violations to some of our members facing charges for burglaries and robberies, and eventually homicide. The alleged murder of police officers would soon take the place of the mythological rape of white women as the basis for the legal lynching of black men.

In April of 1969, James Brown was scheduled to appear on behalf of Richard Nixon in what was billed as a "Decency Rally" at Baltimore's Memorial Stadium. Needless to say, there was little decency involved in this event, and, in a sense, it was little more than a case of the government trying to use music as a distraction to soothe the "savage breast." The stadium was jam-packed with people and so we, the local chapter of the BPP, saw this as an ideal opportunity to speak with them. A similar rally had been held in Miami, Florida and several others were scheduled to happen around the country. There was a sort of Woodstock atmosphere in the air even though we were in urban America, which had suddenly become black America. The people were relaxed and waiting even though it was ninety degrees in the shade on this particular day. We waited and waited but James Brown failed to emerge, and as the sun took its toll, people started to get restless.

Well, after about two hours of waiting, we Panthers, along with anti-war activists and other progressive groups, tried to negotiate some time on the mic until James Brown arrived. This brought a massive and immediate response from the security guards and we were forced to leave the centerfield staging area. Our group then decided to march around the walls of the stadium; we shouted slogans and interacted with the crowd. We started off with about a hundred people but soon the group grew much larger. The officials who organized the rally did not like this and we were expelled after a verbal confrontation. About an hour after we left the stadium, the rally turned into major riot when it became apparent that James Brown was a no-show. People who were both hot *and* angry as they filed out of the stadium were met with hostility as the police aggressively forced the crowd to disperse. As tempers flared, fights broke out and crowds blocked the main thoroughfare, only to be charged or trampled by police on horseback. They were swinging their batons from above and knocking people over; in some cases they rode right over the people who fell down in the mad rush that ensued. It was a disaster and perhaps the most indecent "Decency Rally" ever staged, but fortunately this became the last one that the government attempted to hold.

The presence of the Panthers and our attempt to speak to the crowd became connected with the riot, even though it occurred over an hour after we had left, and was largely the result of people being mistreated by the police after waiting in the heat for a performer who did not materialize. Suddenly, things started happening around our chapter office on different levels. First, our electricity was cut off and the company claimed it was a billing error. Next, a twenty-four-hour surveillance post was set up across the street from us and the police began to tail all known Panther vehicles in both unmarked cars and regular patrol cars. Ultimately, they managed to infiltrate our organization at a number of levels, and though we were unaware of who these "agents" might be at the time, we knew infiltration was a very real possibility.

Despite these setbacks, we held our first successful rally. It took place at Clifton Park on Malcolm X's birthday and drew over a thousand people. The program consisted largely of several speakers from the BPP, followed by a bull roast. The rally was really the first time that the police made themselves fully visible to us after weeks of "covert" harassment. The park was overrun with a massive number of policemen in uniforms and a large number of plainclothes men photographing the participants. Many of these men who were sworn to uphold the law spent their time inventing incidents among the crowd that led to harassment, and eventually spread to people simply walking near the rally site; we eventually dispersed because we did not have a permit.

While we were committed to education, and knew the value of such books as *The Wretched of the Earth*, by Frantz Fanon, the BPP leadership had long believed that the best way to advance our communities was to *actively* address the problems that existed. One of our early efforts was a food co-op that allowed us to provide low-cost groceries for the community while netting enough profit to cover party expenses. Another project that eventually was picked up by others outside the party was the People's Health Clinic located on Greenmount Avenue. The clinic is still in existence today and provides inexpensive healthcare to the uninsured.

Almost every BPP chapter in the country had developed a free breakfast program in their community to feed hungry children. We started our program after polling the neighborhood for miles around our office to see if such a need existed and if a program would receive support from community members if we started it. Once we were convinced that the community was strongly supportive of such a program, we began to contact individuals and organizations that might help us locate a site from which to operate. Help came from a community-based church order. We were given the use of the basement of the St. Martin de Porres Community Center, which was a couple of miles from our main office. We all pitched in to paint and clean the place and many people from the community also came out to help us. They were mostly children, but some parents pitched in to help as well.

We expanded the committee assigned to manage the breakfast program, inviting members of the community to join, both youth and adults. BPP members made contact with as many stores in the area as possible, and each of these businesses were asked to donate anything they could to aid in development of this program. Many of the business owners felt that the program was a good idea and much needed in the community, so they willingly gave as much as they reasonably could, in the form of food, paper plates, and other supplies required to feed large numbers of children. There were, of course, some neighborhood store-owners who refused to aid the program. We assigned teams to investigate those stores and find out how much money they were making off of the community. The stores that took money from the community but gave nothing back were subjected to a community boycott.

Armed with the information about their profits and lack of return to the black community, we put signs up in the area exposing these businesses and then established pickets in front of these places. This brought a quick response from most of the hold-outs. However, true to capitalist form, some still would not contribute resources to feed the hungry children in the community. We kept the pressure up on these stores until we were forced to stop the boycotts on our own because the community youth were starting to get a bit violent toward these stores and the owners were blaming us and the boycotts for these actions.

Of course it never occurred to the owners that the youth in the community might legitimately feel some anger toward them for refusing to support a program that was designed to feed those same youth. And, the local papers came down on the side of the owners and the police, and continued to harass the Panthers in their pages. Nevertheless, the program proved to be successful and it eventually grew so large that we had to go to bigger businesses to get enough food and supplies to meet the rising need. Teams went out with information packages to request support from larger companies and many of them gave whatever they could. The only reason the program had to be limited was time and personnel. You can feed only so many children in a given time and space. Our numbers ranged from between twenty-five to one hundred children a day.

Every morning, five days a week, we opened the place up, cleaned it, and set up the tables. Around 8AM, we would start cooking and the children would also begin to arrive. We had cars that picked up the children who lived a mile or more away from the program. There were always a number of parents and sisters and brothers from the community to stay with the children until the food was ready. We fed everyone there, adults and children alike. When the first group of kids had finished, they were driven to school and the next group would be brought in to start the process over again. Since Kay and I both worked nights, we would go straight to the breakfast program when we got off from work. She would cook and I would drive the children back and forth between the program and school.

There was always real pressure on supporters to stop assisting the program. A 1969 memo from J. Edgar Hoover to twenty-four FBI offices stated: "the free breakfast program represents the best and most influential activity going for the BPP and as such is potentially the greatest threat to efforts by authorities to neutralize the BPP and destroy what it stands for." Shortly thereafter, the now infamous coloring book program was started by the FBI to discredit Black Panther breakfast programs across the country. Some weeks later, odd things began to happen within our chapter. A few people would leave the office to go somewhere and they would be arrested en route and kept overnight on an investigation of some alleged crime. Groups of Black Panthers would go out to attend different events such as a rally or speaking engagement, and of the ten members who might go only eight would return. No one would know what had happened to the other two people until they showed up the next day mad as hell because they had been left behind or had engine failure out on some lonely highway. Our cars were starting to break down on a regular basis.

Finally, when one of our buildings caught fire, I was put in charge of security for the Baltimore chapter and this included the welfare of our members as well as the buildings. All special events had to be checked out and all new individuals coming into the chapter were scrutinized. I spent a lot of time just checking out the backgrounds of people who were interested in joining the party or working close to us. There was also the monumental task of finding out about the people who were already in the party, this included finding out who was working where, and what they were doing. It became a continual process of checking on a number of people and things at any given time. I soon became aware that we had some serious internal problems and it was likely that they had existed right from the inception of the Baltimore chapter.

With the number of incidents that were occurring regularly, it was clear that there were agents operating inside the chapter. There were many times when I reported security violations to the Defense Captain, Warren Hart, but all too often no action was taken to deal with the problem or to investigate the situation any further. The problems continued to escalate, and we lost two more cars, not to mention the fact that our members were still being left here and there at random. Finally, during an open house gathering at our headquarters, we caught someone photographing the inside of the offices in areas that shouldn't have been open to the public. When I inquired with Hart, he told me that he had authorized this action.

I felt compelled to take my concerns to a higher level, because at that point it was impossible to tell who among the local leadership was really on our side. It had become obvious that our branch had been infiltrated by government agents, but where the infiltration started and stopped was still unclear. National headquarters agreed to send us a team of investigators. The regional Field Marshal from New York, Donald Cox, who was responsible for operations on the east coast, brought his own team down to investigate the information that had been gathered, and to hold hearings. Warren Hart and several other people were tried. I had been called out to Oakland and so I was not present, but when I returned several people were gone. We would eventually discover that our Defense Captain, who was the highest-ranking Panther in the state of Maryland, was a paid agent of the National Security Agency. Several other "members" were working for other law enforcement agencies, one for the FBI, two for the local police department, and another for some agency whose name remains unknown. They had been working both individually and collectively as information gatherers and agent provocateurs, and had successfully set up a number of our members on various charges. These activities created a climate of fear and suspicion that left our chapter seriously wounded, and this situation wasn't limited to Baltimore. Similar activities were taking place in most of our chapters around the country. National progressive movements were shifting their stance from the belief that this country's problems were simply the result of racism or capitalism. The government's reaction to our movements resulted in a new form of fascism that was uniquely American: operating under the guise of law and order.

In July 1969, a national conference was organized in Oakland, California to form a united front to combat fascism. Representatives from every state and several different organizations besides the Black Panther Party attended this conference. The Panthers on the east coast used New York as our jumping-off point. We had at that time chapters from Halifax, Nova Scotia to Raleigh, North Carolina, but all the chapters who had people going by the northern route left from New York. Our small caravan consisted of about four cars full of brothers and sisters looking very much like Black Panthers with the berets and black leather jackets. For me, the sojourn was a study in the many facets of black culture as we made our way across the country stopping in most of the major cities along the way. Each time, we would go into the black community and check out the local chapter or simply the community.

The striking similarity between the communities left me believing that you could fall asleep in one ghetto and wake up in another city, inside the black community, and never realize you were in a different state. To see this with my own eyes convinced me that the blight and utter impoverishment that we were seeing had to be the result of a national policy of neglect supported by a capitalist agenda that rendered poor people useless as more and more jobs disappeared from their communities. Everywhere I looked I saw the same liquor stores and bars, dilapidated housing, and young men on the corners, and *always* the excessive policing. The only variation that existed was among the people themselves. They ran the full range of color from high yellow to blue black, and spoke with their various regional dialects. This to me was a reflection of the true beauty and diversity that exists among black people.

Unfortunately, I missed the opportunity to meet Fred Hampton because when we were passing through Chicago I had elected to find a secluded place to teach Zayd Shakur how to drive a stick shift. We had set out with twelve people in our caravan, but only a handful of us could drive and even fewer could operate a stick and, of course, one of the vehicles was a Volkswagen bug—a necessary prop on the set of the 1970s, or so it seems to us these days. Of all of the New York members of the BPP, Zayd was the person with whom I had been most acquainted. I stayed with him whenever I went to New York to train with party members there. He was an intelligent cat who was light years ahead of the Reparations movement in regards to getting money from the government. So while others went to meet the members of the Chicago chapter, I sat in a jerking car giving advice as Zayd tried to get the routine down.

By the time we reached Oakland and the conference site, it was very clear that we had a real problem, and soon an open debate about fascism in America took place. In 1969, some groups and key individuals on the left took the position that the US could not be a fascist state because of the two-party system. They pointed out that there were no secret police nor any centralization of the government or of wealth, while others believed that there was no real opposition between the two major political parties. For many of us Panthers, though, everything in our own collective experience pointed to a system designed to repress and ultimately eliminate our freedom; in fact, our liberty had always been questionable when juxtaposed against capitalism. For me, this was what our struggle was really about, and coupled with the hospitality extended to us by members of the Oakland chapter, I left with a strong sense of community and collectivism. John Seale, brother of Bobby Seale (who would eventually become the BPP Chairman) and his family were very accommodating to us. Several of the comrades and I had come from warm climates and our choice of clothing reflected this. Well, John and others provided us with clothing that was more appropriate to Oakland's chill, in addition to housing and food.

Our trip came to an abrupt end when members of the New York chapter had to rush back to deal with a situation there. Some comrades who had been out on bail had been rounded up when two others had apparently jumped bail. Hard as it may be to believe, we made it back in about sixty-two hours; I guess those driving lessons had paid off.

We could not have known it then, but the country would soon learn that the FBI and other state and local agencies were in fact functioning as a national secret police, but, unfortunately, by the time that information became public, many of us would have already fallen victim to these covert operations. Without a doubt, the wealth in the US was then, and has remained, centralized, and historically anyone who ever presented any real opposition to the status quo has suffered horrendous consequences. The government spies and agent provocateurs continued both day and night to follow, record, harass, and set-up individuals and groups who opposed the state on the issues of human, civil, and economic rights for the poor and oppressed groups.

The intention of COINTELPRO, the so-called "Counter Intelligence Program," was to coordinate the activities of federal, state, and local intelligence and law enforcement agencies in an effort to dismantle FBI designated targets. The targets were originally supposed to be foreign agent networks, but the mark rapidly became American citizens—both individuals and groups. The FBI controlled—directly and indirectly—thousands of informers and agent provocateurs, who engaged in everything from simple misinformation to sabotage and murder in the course of their work for government agencies. When the FBI office in Media, Pennsylvania was compromised on March 8, 1971 and classified files ended up in the hands of the news media, the FBI's COINTELPRO operations suddenly became public. That discovery was followed by a Freedom of Information Act (FOIA) lawsuit that produced more evidence demonstrating the programs' scope. Officially, COINTELPRO operated from 1956 to 1971. Unofficially, the program continued under other names, and was most recently codified as the USA PATRIOT Act.

The final report of April 23, 1976 from the senate intelligence committee (known as the Church Committee) that was assigned to investigate the program states that "the chief investigative branch of the federal government (FBI) which was charged by law with investigating crimes and preventing criminal conduct itself engaged in lawless tactics and responded to deep seated social problems by fomenting violence and unrest" (see my book *The Greatest Threat*, 102). In reality, COINTELPRO was a product of American-style national fascism; it may not have been as overt as German, Italian, Argentine, or Spanish fascism, but it existed—and still exists today—in the United States. The Black Panther Party had already recognized that it was the target of fascist attacks, authorized and overseen by the government itself. America was, for the Panthers, little more than a police state: the violation of rights, the orders for law enforcement officers to break or cross the laws they are sworn to uphold, the cold-blooded murder of individuals in the name of those laws, and the spreading of hate and terror as policing tactics ... these are the daily functions of a police state.

Of the 295 actions carried out against "black nationalist hate groups" under the auspices of the Counter-Intelligence Program between 1967 and 1971, 233 of them were directed against the Black Panther Party. As internal documents reveal, the FBI employed its most vicious tactics in the disruption/disinformation operations against the Panthers (see Ward Churchill and Jim Vander Wall, *The COINTELPRO Papers*, 164). Shortly after Richard Nixon took office in January 1969, his top aides addressed themselves, in the words of ex-White House counsel John Dean, "to the matter of how we can maximize the fact of our incumbency in dealing with persons known to be active in their opposition to our administration ... stated a bit more bluntly ... how we can use the available federal machinery to screw our political enemies." To that end, a White House enemies list was drawn up by Nixon's officials. For the FBI, CIA, IRS, NSA, and other federal agencies that would eventually receive the list, this was a sign that the race to destroy any opposition to the political status quo had already begun and had just been accepted and approved by the highest echelons of the American government.

The National Conference to Combat Fascism had been successful in highlighting most of these signs of a growing American fascism at a governmental level, and as a result many new organizations were cropping up across the nation. At the same time, the fascist backlash was strong, and the response quickly began to take its toll on the black community and on radical left groups in general. Nationally, the ties and connections between black and white groups on the left had begun to weaken by 1969; our experience working with white radicals in Baltimore was a case in point. The Panthers suspected that the federal government was coordinating attacks on the party and individual chapters, and for this reason had called for the conference to address this tide of repression. The anti-war movement in Baltimore was small but very active from 1968 to 1970, and the main organization that the Panthers worked with was Peace Action. We had formed a loose network that encompassed several other groups, including the Catonsville Nine and people from that regional network. There was also a newly developing White Panther Party, which we were relating to. Our members spent many hours in the offices of these different groups, and invested a lot of time supporting their rallies and demonstrations, but there were always underlying problems in dealing with the local white organizations.

Besides some of the basic, and not unexpected, differences around goals and objectives, there existed the very real problem of drug use among some members of the anti-war movement—on a twenty-four-hour basis. Though some of our members drank and smoked a little marijuana from time to time, the days of wild abandonment and overindulgence in the earliest days of the Panther Party in Baltimore were long since over. Assassinations of our members and infiltrations of our offices around the country had imbued our work with a new seriousness; getting high was not all that cool with us when our lives were on the line twenty-four-hours a day. Because of the attacks on Panther offices, we often had arms among us and no one trusted anyone who was under the influence of drugs around the firearms.

There was also the problem of race relations, since so many of our members had come to the BPP by way of some of the Black Nationalist movements and organizations, or held pro-nationalist views that were deeply ingrained. This made trust among the groups rather difficult, despite efforts on both sides to change these attitudes. And finally, there was the resultant anger caused by relationships between black men and white women, a result of the "free love" concepts of the white radical movement. Eventually one such relationship between a member of the party and the wife of a white lawyer sympathetic to the cause would become a source of provocation for the FBI who circulated a false letter making public the infidelity.

Many sisters in the BPP openly opposed these relationships, as did some community supporters, and I am certain that a similar position was held by some of the white male radicals. Several sisters conveyed the belief that these relationships were taking available black men away from them while brothers tended to overlook their concerns about these relationships.

The sum total of all these problems made it impossible to establish anything other than a loosely-structured supportive network between black and white activists. There was a wide and disparate level of representation from the black community; membership in the party ranged from street hustlers or the lumpen, to college students and academics. On the other hand, the majority of the white activists who we encountered in the anti-war movement were of a privileged class. Whites who were at an economic advantage had the privilege of devoting time to the movement; poor whites and blacks were not afforded such convenience. With this distinction of class also came white supremacy and the unconscious racism that has always existed among less-politicized white radicals. This was reflected in their attempts to run, direct, or lead everything we were jointly involved in, which resulted in an immediate backlash from our members almost every time, and at every point. The relationship we shared with the old-guard left, and by this I mean the American Communist Party, and labor and union organizers, was even more distant than our relationship to New Left groups like Students for a Democratic Society, the Young Socialist Workers Party, and the White Panther Party.

There seemed to be a more concrete exchange with the old left in a number of areas, but there was never any real trust between us because we believed that they had sold out by becoming middle-class Americans, while they tended to believed that we were young crazy blacks who might do anything at any time. They gave us support in many areas, but kept a good distance from us and our activities. But, on the whole, among the various leftist groups, there was a real effort to defend the movement from the continued attacks by the right-wing of the American government.

The rapid growth of the BPP, after a number of armed actions on the west coast, was as much responsible for its decline as anything else. The fact that this allowed thousands of new members to flood the ranks of each chapter, while ill-trained personnel were allowed to open new chapters with little or no real guidance, led to problems in maintaining uniformity and collective policies. The new influx of members were, for the most part, accepted after the death of Dr. King, and these members had recently come through the wave of riots that swept America's cities after King's assassination. Most were angry as hell and ready to fight the system on any level. There were more new members than the old comrades could safely absorb. This was the time of the government's greatest efforts to infiltrate their agents into the party.

It seems that every law enforcement agency from local, state, and national levels placed their agents within not only the Black Panther Party, but also any other progressive group on the political terrain, although there seemed to be special orders about catalyzing violence and conflict among the Panthers in particular. A number of organizations were developing at the time, but the BPP was at the top of the list for removal or disruption. Closely following the BPP for that honor were the Brown Berets, the American Indian Movement, the Young Lords, the White Panthers, SDS, and the anti-war movement. The Black Panther Party was making a serious effort to bring all these groups together under the United Front to Combat Fascism.

The government, of course, was prepared to do everything in its power to stop us from uniting around a common cause. They made significant use of the media, often feeding publications stories that discredited the Panthers. Differences in race and politics provided a variety of angles from which to target the different groups and disrupt organizing efforts. Their misinformation campaigns helped to nurse latent doubts that existed within these groups about who was using whom and for what purpose. The media, for example, did their best to paint a misleading picture of internal conflicts between the leadership of the BPP, in the hopes of destabilizing the BPP's entire base of operations. Yet, chapters continued to grow and expand, even in the face of repeated attacks by law enforcement, the media, and right-wing organizations.

The negative press was actually serving as a recruitment tool for us. Many people were attracted to the BPP because of the negative media images. They would sometimes try to actualize their ideas about revenge and violence, and this made them prime victims for agent provocateurs within the ranks of the local and national organizational structure. It was about this time that the national government decided that it was time to get in on the kill publicly. They did this by holding a number of well-publicized congressional hearings, spearheaded by the so-called House Committee on Un-American Activities, which called a number of law enforcement officials to testify before nationwide television networks and paint a picture of the Black Panther Party as wild, crazy niggers who ate babies. This hideous show was designed to prepare the public for the coming attacks against the party—attacks designed to completely disrupt the BPP and shatter its leadership once and for all. So these hearings focused on two aspects of the party: the internal treatment of its members and the external relationship with the community. First to be used in this effort were a husband and wife team of so-called ex-Panthers in full uniforms. No one had ever heard of them, but that never mattered before. They testified that the BPP forced them to stay in the party and to do a lot of things that were against their principles. They saw the rape of young teenage girls by BPP members, and described massive drug use and armed robberies by the party leadership.

The second level of attack was directed at the breakfast program. This is where the now-infamous coloring book (a coloring book that was supposed to teach little children how to kill policemen) was presented on national television as a product of the BPP's breakfast program. The fact that this book was designed, produced, and distributed by the FBI would be proven later, but the damage was done. They mailed it to companies that had supported the program with donations of food. Groups and individuals began to withdraw their building or material support for the breakfast programs. The fact that the United States Congress was reporting these things meant that most average Americans believed them. In time, most states would implement free lunch programs in the schools, and eventually add free breakfast programs, since, as the Panthers had demonstrated, much to the chagrin of the political leaders of the country, these were resources sorely needed in communities across the nation. In Baltimore, the Maryland Food Committee was set up to undermine the BPP's nutrition program because it promoted self-determination in the black community. The local black churches that moved in to fill the program's needs were suddenly being supplied with federal funds to do so.

Shortly after these media attacks began, the government began to mount much more deadly offensives. One of the first occurred in Chicago, and it would result in the silencing of one of the party's key organizers in that city, Illinois Chairman Fred Hampton. The mood in our office in December 1969 was one of shock and anger over the news that was trickling out of Chicago. Initial reports said a number of Black Panthers had been shot and wounded in a shoot-out with police while resisting arrest in a pre-dawn raid. However, the word from our national headquarters was that Chairman Fred had been assassinated in his sleep by a combined team of state, local, and federal enforcement agents; he had just become a member of the BPP Central Committee, the national body governing the party.

We were certain that the long-awaited attacks had started, and now the realization had begun to sink in that it wouldn't be long before the fate of many of our comrades would befall us as well. As the details of what happened in Chicago continued to trickle in, our members moved around the office as if a wake were taking place. We had not gotten beyond this tragedy, had no time to consider a defense, when we received news of yet another attack on our national leadership. Bobby Seale had been arrested and shipped to New Haven, Connecticut on trumped up murder charges. Yet another national leader was being removed from the Central Committee by the reactionary forces of the government. Things looked very dismal at that moment, but my political resolve remained intact even as my personal life was beginning to unravel. It was enough to have to realize that we were facing opposition from a government that intended to squash our movement, but on top of that, to be confronted with the loss of so many comrades, so many young people who would never see the future they were working to impact … it was too much. I'm sure that my family members feared for my well being, and the responsibilities that came along with my commitment to the Panthers were affecting my relationship with Kay, who simply needed more than I could give.

John Huggins and Bunchy Carter had been assassinated the year before in Los Angeles; Eldridge Cleaver was in exile in Cuba, having fled falsified charges resulting from the confrontation with the Oakland police who had summarily executed Little Bobby Hutton; and Huey Newton was essentially fighting for his life in California, though he would later be released. Now Fred Hampton had been assassinated in his sleep. We were losing community support while these attacks were being stepped up, and guidance and management of party affairs had been truncated. Black community leaders, the type that are usually appointed by City Hall, and only speak out about things when there is a problem that City Hall wants talked about, were suddenly talking their heads off.

By the following week, news reached us that the FBI had asked the Baltimore City police to get indictments for the leadership of our chapter. They were saying one of their informants was missing and he was supposed to be working out of one of our offices. We had seen and known this brother they were talking about, so we checked out his whereabouts with his sister. She told us that she had talked to him two weeks before and that he was being sent somewhere by the company he worked for. The FBI claimed he was missing for over 3 months.

A similar charge was being leveled at Bobby Seale and Ericka Huggins up in New Haven, Connecticut. It was yet another missing informant case that would prove to be an attempt to frame the BPP leadership. We discussed the situation with our lawyer and decided to wait until they took some type of action. In the meantime, we gathered as much information as we could about what was going on. Up front, it seemed as if they had infiltrated one of their agents into our chapter and eventually just sent him elsewhere, or instructed him to hide; but the Baltimore City police had other ideas. Leakin Park in West Baltimore has always had some notoriety, primarily because of the number of bodies that have been dumped there over the years. It seemed to yield more bodies than some local cemeteries and this became very convenient for the local police. They used one of these unidentified bodies to move on our leadership in the chapter, claiming that it was the remains of an informant who had been killed by several members. It became known as the "bag of bones" case; the remains would soon be identified as belonging to a white male. All of the members who were charged with this murder would eventually be acquitted, except for one who chose to accept a plea deal early on in the case. He would later receive a pardon from the governor. Since all the people we worked with were informed and believed an attack was the real motive behind this whole set-up, we continued to work but stayed on the defensive since attacks were being directed at almost every chapter across the nation. Less than two weeks later another attack came, but it occurred away from our office and involved a member who the police claimed was involved in a robbery attempt. The result was a dead Panther, a brother by the name of Drummond. The facts were murky at best so I investigated it with the people in the neighborhood where the shooting had occurred and their story was very different from the one being told by the police. The media was on strike that week, so it was not covered and eventually it went down as a justified police shooting and that was that.

By the time Fred Hampton was murdered in his sleep, Kay and I were no longer living together. I had moved to a neighborhood in West Baltimore and she had taken Ronald and moved to New York. Our marriage had been fraught with conflict, in part due to her own personal issues, but largely due to the fact that I had often placed more importance on the struggle than my own family. It had been my belief that by making conditions better in the community I would also make things better for my family. In retrospect, my activism made things worse—our family was broken and Ronald would grow up without his father around. Since returning from the service, I had also been the glue that had held my extended family together, and in a few short years, this would also be irrevocably altered. These days, I can tell you that the greatest regret of my life is the fact that I wasn't there for so many people, including my children and my mother, during some of the roughest years of their lives. But back then, despite being married and being a parent, I was still young and selfish. None of those things were as important to me as *me* and what *I* wanted. And what I wanted was bigger than family; it was freedom for myself and my people.

regret   the pull of activism over family

Chapter Five

Door of No Return

In addition to the murder of Fred Hampton, the beginning of December 1969 had brought with it the chilly news of an all-day siege upon the Los Angeles office. The firefight involved armored cars and helicopters, and launched the newly-formed SWAT (Special Weapons and Tactics) Team, an ultra-militarized police unit in Los Angeles that would soon filter out into police precincts across the country. This was, of course, a pre-dawn attack, which seemed to be the *modus operandi* for these kinds of offensives, and it resulted in a number of injuries and 18 arrests, among them two more Central Committee members.

By this point, the Baltimore chapter had begun to implement a number of strategies to counteract the attacks we were experiencing. Members had been working to establish chapters in Washington D.C., Reading, Pennsylvania, and Wilmington, Delaware. Members from the Baltimore chapter were dispatched to each of these regions, and they would bring back new recruits to our offices to be trained. The chapters in D.C. and Delaware would ultimately grow and develop into active organizations that survived longer than any of Maryland's chapters. Back home, there was an office in East Baltimore, one in South Baltimore, and another one in Annapolis, with plans to establish a new one in West Baltimore. This was the last area of Baltimore to be organized. The Panthers had been in the area for some time already selling newspapers and holding small rallies when we decided to move our main office to Pennsylvania Avenue, which was, and still is, one of the main arteries on the west side. A few of us also moved to the area and began to seek out a good location for our new office.

Our newspaper sales were increasing in the community and residents wanted to know when we would start some programs there. There had been an increase in police violence in the area—we witnessed two major block-wide police raids within a three-month period, in which everyone on the street was held and searched by the infamous tactical squads that the police department had put in place to conduct raids in what they deemed "nuisance" areas. To me, it called up images of Nazi Germany, because it was becoming increasingly clear that neither the Constitution, nor the Bill of Rights, nor any of those other documents that claim liberty and justice for all were worth the paper they were written on. Human rights were violated all the time in poor communities like Sandtown and Uptown, where our main office was about to be relocated. In no time at all, incidents between police and neighborhood youth led to a mini-riot, and in the aftermath there was a shootout that led to the deaths of a brother who lived in the neighborhood and a policeman. Police claimed the shootings were the result of a drug raid; the Panthers had been negotiating for the lease on a building a block away from the site of the incident.

The following week there was a shooting a few blocks in the other direction; one police officer was killed and another wounded. The blame for this incident was laid at the feet of the Panthers. From what we could gather from the police reports, a patrol car had been dispatched investigate a disturbance at a house in the area sometime during the night. The officers left, but were later called back and the shooting occurred soon after their return. Not long after that, we heard that two of our members had been arrested near the site of these shootings and they were being held. I was subsequently arrested at my job, and held for the earlier FBI indictments involving the missing informant. My arrest occurred two days after the shootings, and in the course of the next few days some 24 members of our chapter would be arrested on various charges ranging from possession of arms to murder to interstate flight. This was the long-expected final assault on the entire leadership of our chapter. The defense captain was kidnapped by agents from California, our main office was set on fire, and many of our members' apartments were raided, resulting in the loss of most of the chapter's political materials and records, many of which were removed from the office by the Baltimore City Fire Department and turned over to the police. Upon arrest, all of our members were placed in a special section of the Baltimore City Jail, the lockup and punishment unit. A few of our members were held in secret at other jails in an attempt to make them appear to be informants or to disguise the fact that they were. I was held as an accessory before and after the fact in the murder of an FBI informant.

After being held for two months with no real evidence against me the judge in the case ordered the State's Attorney to release me or give a better reason for holding me. During this time, the state was holding Jack Johnson and attempting to get him to testify against me. Not so co-incidentally, an informant was transferred into my cell. Charles Reynolds was recognized by other prisoners who had served time with him in the Maryland House of Corrections. Some of these men were in the receiving area when he was processed into the jail, and sent word to me that an informer was being assigned to my cell. I would later find out that, through an arrangement with Baltimore City police department, he was being transported from the Jessup, Maryland prison complex to serve out the balance of his time in Michigan, where he was from. This was an unusual move for a prisoner coming from a maximum security prison and being sent to another state to serve out time because the Baltimore City Jail was a minimum security facility where prisoners served short sentences or were held pending trail and sentencing. Prisoners from a state prison were generally transferred directly from one state's facility to the next state. I was aware that they were trying to build a case against me on the police shootings, but I wasn't all that concerned at the time because I was innocent. When the word came up that a police informant was being specifically assigned to the cell I was in, though, I knew I had a problem. I thought maybe the government wanted me to attack him or have someone attack him so that they could continue holding me as a threat to the community. I also knew that this informant was being placed there to build a case against me in the police shootings, and so I protested his placement in my cell. The guards refused to place him in another cell, saying that they had their orders.

I would later learn that the Baltimore City police commissioner, a man named Pommerlau, had been called to Washington D.C. to meet with Attorney General John Mitchell, who, according to the newspaper reports, was under orders to make the charges against us stick, whatever the cost. With that in mind, a number of things happened around the same time. First, the police informant was eventually removed from my cell and shipped to Michigan to serve out a sentence there, but he would later give a statement implicating me, in exchange for favorable recommendations from the State's Attorney's office concerning his sentence in Michigan. Next, Jackie Johnson, one of the two Panthers arrested almost immediately following the shootings gave a statement against me under the agreement that he receive immunity from prosecution. Once on the stand, he would refuse to testify, so the statement was not be used in the trial. I would find out later that Jack's statement was the result of beatings and intimidation by the police. And finally, a police officer who was involved in the aftermath of the shooting claimed he could identify me because I had been living in the neighborhood surrounding Pennsylvania Avenue all of my life. This came as complete surprise to me since I had only moved there in the last six months, around the time we decided to put an office on the west side.

When finally I went to court on these charges, the trial lasted seven days. I recall very little about it since I spent the entire time in the bullpen (the lockup section for the court). I had been fighting a losing battle with the judge and D.A. about having a lawyer from the Black Panther Party represent me in the case. I'd had problems with the lawyer situation since my arrest. Milton B. Allen, who was one of the best black lawyers in the city at the time, came to see me on the pretense that he was considering representing my case. We talked for about an hour and he left, after assuring me that he would get back to me. He never returned to see me again, and it wasn't a week later that I learned that he had been offered an opportunity to run for State's Attorney. In fact, he was the State's Attorney during the time I was tried. I always wondered how much of what I discussed with him went to his assistants.

By that point, I had realized I couldn't trust any lawyers in the city because they were subject to pressure and bribes as a part of the establishment with their future interests at stake, so I decided that I had to get a political lawyer since this was a political case receiving real dirty political treatment. I would try to get a lawyer from the regional area office, which was located in New York. The Black Panther Party was financially in trouble because of the massive amounts of money being drained from it in the form of bail and legal fees for other members around the country.

Since I had been locked up, some twenty or more attacks had taken place in different cities, each one resulting in arrests and bails or future trials. Part of the government's attack upon the party had been to lock up as many members as possible to keep the party's funds depleted. This ploy was in full-swing by the time of my arrest, and the membership was chipping in to help bail arrested comrades out of jail.

The real source of money for the chapters was from the sale of our newspapers, and that was under attack also. The Maryland state chapter was having real problems with the newspaper at the local airport end of things. Each week, they would lose or misplace thousands of our newspapers. The newspapers a chapter received made it possible to pay the rent for the office space and feed the children and party members sometimes. Many members didn't have paying jobs and lived off the funds they earned selling the newspapers. The continued loss of paper sales cost the chapter great sums of money. Only later was it revealed that this was another attack orchestrated by the FBI.

A later-released memo from FBI headquarters made it clear that the government believed that the Black Panther Party newspaper was one of the most effective propaganda operations of the Party—and they were right. But the memo didn't stop there: "Distribution of this newspaper is increasing at a regular rate," it went on, "thereby influencing a greater number of individuals in the United States along the black extremist lines. Each recipient submitted proposed counterintelligence measures which will hinder the vicious propaganda being spread by the BPP.... The newspaper is the voice of the BPP and if it could be effectively hindered it would result in helping to cripple the Black Panther Party." Well, so much for the freedom of the press and the first amendment rights of US citizens! In any case, that sure didn't seem to apply to blacks. In January 1970, the main distribution center for the Black Panther newspaper in San Francisco was hit by an arson fire that destroyed tens of thousands of papers. Because of these continued attacks from the government agencies, our members' legal defense fund was greatly limited. Along with the mounting legal costs there was also a real shortage of political lawyers. An extraordinary number of movement people were under attack in America at the same time, and lawyers were needed by the anti-war groups, the American Indian Movement, the radical student movements, the Puerto Rican independence movement, the Mexican-American movement, the left church movement, and the prison movement. There simply were not enough lawyers to go around. And, besides that, the political lawyers themselves were under attack, meaning that less and less of them were able or willing to carry on in the courts. It's safe to say there was a waiting list a mile long to get a political lawyer. I was waiting for one of them myself. While I was waiting, though, I had to get some things done on my situation.

We hired a city lawyer to deal with these things, with the understanding that as soon as we got a political lawyer he or she would handle the case. I was to be assigned a lawyer from William Kuntsler's office in New York. After this was explained to the judge, he assigned a public defender to the case with the understanding that I was waiting on the lawyer out of New York who would be handling the case. The judge asked for proof of this, so William Kuntsler appeared in court to explain all of this in person. He requested thirty days to get his law partner down to Baltimore. The lawyer was in the middle of another case and needed time to finish it. The judge agreed, and then despite this agreement, scheduled the trial for three days later with the public defender I'd only met with three times, and only for fifteen minutes on those occasions.

Later, a prominent Baltimore attorney would state to my supporters that Mr. McAllister was placed on the case because he had some level of credibility. But, he said, by that point in his career McAllister was no longer competent; he had become an alcoholic, and he was sometimes drunk during the trial.

I was not willing to go to a rigged trial with a drunken public defender and I stated that position clearly in court. The judge and D.A. decided to move ahead with the case before a lawyer from Kunstler's firm could come down and get involved. I continued to protest but they went right on with the proceedings. I made it clear that I was not going to allow this court-assigned lawyer to represent me in this case; my life was on the line. I fired him, and the judge continued with the case anyway. He said that he had to make sure I got a fast and speedy trial because it was my right, yet there were brothers over at the City Jail waiting to go to trial for almost two years in some cases. I could see they intended to have a show with or without a lawyer I could trust. At that point I decided that if they were planning a legal lynching I would not step easily into the noose, so I called it what it was: a sham. The least act of resistance, I mean the absolute minimal thing that I could do to resist this, was for me was to leave the courtroom in protest, so I made this point clear and then left.

I only returned to participate in the trial when forced to or when my cell partner, Arthur Turco urged me to. He was one of the BPP's lawyers at the time, and he had been arrested in New York and charged in the informant case in Baltimore and was being held at the jail. During this time, Turco was the Chairman of the Patriot Party, a radical white New Left political party. We had been in the cell together since they had brought him down from New York. He had been advising me on the legal aspects of my case and I had asked the judge on numerous occasions to allow me to use him as my attorney since I could trust him. The judge initially agreed, but later changed his mind. I never doubted for a minute that the judge was under a lot of pressure from someone above him; so much for justice in America. I had no pretense about the fact that American justice was meted out in larger portions for the rich while the poor could only cross their fingers and hope.

Each day, the courtroom was packed with people from the community and this led to a number of threats from the judge about limiting the number of people that would be allowed to watch the trial. I watched each day's proceedings on a local news station at night to find out what had happened that day. Since I wasn't at the trial, I am forced to rely on the transcript of the court proceedings. Many thoughts raced through my mind during the days that the trial went on, but most often I wondered how many other people, poor and black, had come through this same system looking for justice and receiving nothing, not even some good lies. The justice system, just like other institutions in the US, was working night and day to suppress anyone who posed a threat to the rich and powerful of this country. Its sole purpose as far as I could see was to maintain a system that operated in the interest of a small group of criminals like Richard Nixon who were bombing and killing people at that very moment in Cambodia, Vietnam, and even on US college campuses like Jackson State in Mississippi, Kent State in Ohio, and Southern University down in Baton Rouge, Louisiana. All had suffered deaths and injuries during the late sixties and seventies. Thousands of people in the US and around the world were dying because of the international and economic policies directed by a tiny minority—less than one percent of the population—who owned and controlled eighty-five percent of the country's wealth.

These killers used war and genocide as a means of securing a global economy for themselves. I knew that if these folks would kill their own children, like they did at Kent State, they would surely use the heavy hand of government to swat us Panthers like so many roaches. I had no illusions about receiving justice in America. The legal violations that had been perpetrated against me to get a conviction seemed to be so far beyond the bounds of the legal system that I just couldn't understand how normal people could possibly be fooled by the State's actions. But, then again, these very same people had re-elected Nixon and he was a crook. They had elected Agnew and he was a crook. They believed Johnson about the Vietnam War and accepted verbatim the Warren Commission report about the Kennedy Assassination. They even believed Hoover while he was tapping their phones. Apparently they would believe anything, so why not this?

The seven days of my trial demonstrated beyond a shadow of a doubt that this country is indeed a police state. The only people who had a voice during my trial were police, government informers, and government employees. I did not participate and they did not honor my right to choose an attorney. The whole rap back then, like now, was about "law and order." I felt that the whole process was unlawful and quite out of order. Those of us from the BPP, the AIM, and other such movements who were being locked up were, for the most part, raising issues that needed to be addressed in the US. It was, however, the demand for self-determination that posed the greatest threat to the government's agenda. This could put a stop to the oppression and genocide in the black and native communities and even draw the war in Vietnam to an end as people refused to go. It could potentially change conditions for poor and working-class people around the country.

Activists were targeted and locked up, while the people who had stolen vast quantities of the world's resources from the rest of us would continue to do so. The wealthy and powerful summarily broke the same laws that they swore by, violating their own Constitution as well as every civil and human right known to humankind. These wealthy and powerful people would decide who was guilty and who was to be jailed, and in the case of some, who lived and who died. When we charged "genocide," the same people were quick to point out that this was not Nazi Germany. After all, they said, in America we had a justice system in which one was presumed innocent until proven guilty, and an individual had the right to a jury of his or her own peers. There are no gas ovens here, it is true, but genocide is the deliberate destruction of an ethnic group, and the targeting of blacks and native peoples in the United States in those years was certainly that.

The United States of America is still the only major nation in the United Nations that refuses to recognize genocide as a crime (though it was designated as such under international law by the UN General Assembly when it approved the convention on punishment of the crime of genocide in December 1949). It is no wonder when one considers the mass arrests of African descended and native youth, the flooding of these communities with alcohol and drugs rendering them lifeless, and finally the use of sterilization as a birth control practice for women of color. Justice? There is none; I was found guilty after the violation of my constitutional rights, my civil rights, and my human rights. It was pre-determined that I would go to prison while the real crooks went back to their estates to map out the future of the Empire.

Shortly before I was moved from the Baltimore City Jail in February of 1971, there was a major riot, the result of long-ignored concerns over food and visiting conditions in the jail. I had been awaiting the outcome of my appeal and had not yet been moved to a prison. Because of my influence among some of the younger brothers in the jail who viewed me as a leader, I got the blame for this incident along with Arthur Turco. The reality is that when a riot occurs there are usually no actual leaders, only people relieving their frustrations and other people staying out of their way. The afternoon that the riot took place I had been summoned by a guard who said that I had a visit. After spending a mere ten minutes with my visitor, I was told by the guard that my time was up because visiting hours were over. Naturally, I protested, stating my anger to the guard who, it turned out, had deliberately kept my visitor waiting nearly two hours before he decided to bring me up for the visit.

My protestations led to an argument with this guard and we began to scuffle. Soon enough, other prisoners—including the actor Charles Dutton, who was awaiting trial—joined me in the beef, before we knew it, at least a dozen guards were involved. At some point during the al-tercation, a prisoner grabbed a set of keys and opened the cells on the L Wing. The men in that section armed themselves with whatever they could find—mop handles and metal bars—and suddenly it was on. The guards tossed tear gas canisters into the area, but it did not stop the men as they tossed mattresses from the cells and threw trashcans from the upper tier. During the fight with the guards, I had been dragged off to the hole. The other prisoners began negotiating with officials, but refused to compromise until they were made aware of what was happening to me.

For my part, I was stripped naked and thrown into a cold, dank, dark space with a mattress on the floor and a hole in the middle for waste. I had to survive on a diet of water and three sandwiches a day; sometimes they had bologna and sometimes cheese, but never both. I guess I was supposed to be happy for either one, but as time progressed and the stench coming from that hole in the floor engulfed the space, I lost my appetite. They kept me locked in twenty-four hours a day for three weeks until I was transported to the courthouse and sentenced to life plus thirty years. This experience did not break my resolve to resist the repression. It merely awakened me to the world that I had entered and would walk in for years to come. It was such a profound experience that I will probably carry it with me into my next life. When the door slammed on me in the hole, I shuddered because it evoked a strange feeling of déjà vu, but it would be some time before I fully understood this eerily familiar feeling. It was the echo of other doors that offered no return for those who crossed through.

In my mind I could see the faces of those Africans, perhaps even my own ancestors who were forced to cross the threshold of the Door of No Return. I sensed that the people left something of themselves there, caged for eternity. These castles on the coasts of West Africa are all that remain of the people who were snatched away. Those who survived the forced passage would become a different people, of a different mind, with thoughts shaped by the bondage in which they lived. The shadows of who they had been would remain in the ruins of those old castles and the shadows of who they would become are caged here in this country in newly ruined castles called prisons.

I was eventually charged and convicted of assault on the guard. I left the Baltimore City Jail and went directly to the Maryland Penitentiary, an awful structure that is reminiscent of a medieval castle. It is a fortress of sorts, but not one designed to protect its inhabitants. Rather the design of the building has a direct relationship to oppression, from the structure's connection to slavery and the slave trade right on to the present function of warehousing the disappeared from the state's poor black communities.

The penitentiary housed those people who often posed a "threat" to society, runaway black women and men who refused the hand dealt them under slavery, anti-slavery abolitionists and Quakers who interfered with the institution, and those poor whites that did not fit into an economic picture based on slave labor. The first prisoner to cross the threshold of the Maryland Penitentiary in 1811 was a man of African descent named Negro Bob; a rendering of his face and that of his warden grace the stone entryway of the prison. I suspect that the last man out of the door will be of African descent as well.

Chapter Six

Slave Ship

It took most of the day to get processed into the prison. I was confronted with multiple tiers of cells that were filled with nothing but black bodies in cages. Coming out of the isolation of the "hole" at the city jail felt like I had emerged from a dark alley onto a four lane highway. The penitentiary was a swirl of activity: guards changing shifts, prisoners being checked in and processed out, visitors arriving and leaving the place, and civilian employees going back and forth performing their tasks. The time in the "hole" had forced me into quiet reflection and contemplation. I resolved to never give up my struggle for freedom for me or my people, so the penitentiary represented to me just another level of struggle. Though I was now consigned to a life of imprisonment, I had but one immediate thing on my mind: the fact that I had not eaten a full meal in the past twenty-one days had me looking forward to some food.

It was about 5PM before it was time for our section to go to the mess hall. The place was a long square building sitting in the middle of the yard away from all the other buildings in the compound. It was at least a hundred years old, and looked it, both inside and out. Off to the left side near the front and extending toward the center of this huge room were the serving counters. Lined up behind these counters was a row of prisoners dressed in whites.

We filed through this area picking up metal trays and utensils as we passed the deposit points. From that point onward, food was piled upon your tray, depending on whether you kept it on the counter or withdrew it in front of this or that item. Needless to say, I kept my tray upon the counter the full route and the result was a full tray of meat, vegetables, potatoes, bread, and chocolate pudding. I was ready to eat for days. By this point, I may well have lost twenty pounds as a result of the previous three weeks of sandwiches, three times a day, which made up my entire diet. Most of the sandwiches contained meats that I did not eat anyway.

Finally, our section went to sit down at the rows of tables that covered the entire back half of the mess hall. Each row of tables was filled up before the next row was used. The guards would stand at the edge of the tables and direct the prisoner to sit in this seat or that seat, depending on which ones were empty. Up until now, all of my experiences with meals while incarcerated were in the City Jail. As soon as I had arrived at the jail, I was sent to the lockup section, where prisoners are kept in cells at all times including during meals.

There, I could consume my food at my own pace and once I was finished I would put my disposable trays outside. The section clean-up man would collect the containers and clean up the area. Sometimes I would consume my food over the span of several hours depending on what I was doing when the trays got passed out. For example, if I were playing a game of chess with the man in the next cell, the game might last for another hour before someone wins. The food may go untouched the whole time the game is going on.

Now, after living and eating like this for over eleven months, the penitentiary arrangement was a new experience for me. So, as I sat down to eat (and not at a slow pace, as I was truly hungry), I was completely surprised to hear the guard tell everyone, "Okay, that's enough! Let's go!" I watched everyone from my table get up and file out to the trashcan area, and out the door. I never moved, because I still had half a tray of food, and bad teeth to boot. I was really trying to speed things up when a guard stopped in front of me and asked me what I thought I was doing. Well, between mouthfuls, I told him that I was trying to eat my supper, and that I was only half way through and had bad teeth.

By the time I was twenty-one years old and in the army, I had lost half of the teeth in the back of my mouth, and the remaining ones were not in the best of shape. I had learned to always take my time when eating. I quickly learned that I was never again going to have that luxury. Now I was supposed to do what the guards told me to do. Thinking about the situation now, I suppose I must have been some sight, even in a prison. Sitting there eating like a starving man, funky because I had not had a shower in three weeks, my hair was long and uncombed from being in the hole all that time. And because of the weight loss, I had an emaciated appearance. My transfer to the penitentiary had afforded me my first look in the mirror in three weeks and it was a shock.

The guard said that my meal was over and that I had to go. I really didn't understand any of this at the time; it just didn't make any sense. Why give people food to eat and then make them throw half of it away? Well, that will never make sense to a hungry man, and at that time that's just what I was. The whole time that this was happening I had not missed a beat in my eating, nor was I making any effort to be rebellious. I just simply wanted to finish my meal and return to my cell, as I was exhausted from the day's activities. The next thing I knew there were ten to fifteen guards at my table telling me that I'd better hurry up or else. Well, my mouth was full and I had another spoonful of food waiting for an opening. So, I felt like I was doing my best. I knew that something was going wrong here, and after upwards of thirty prisoners started to mill around the guards and started making statements like, "Leave him alone," and "Let the man eat," I knew that there was a situation developing here and it was starting to involve more people than myself.

I decided to finish my meal, or rather declare that I had had enough and move out. I did that for a number of reasons. First, I had no way of knowing just what was going on with the meal situation. It was my first day in the penitentiary and I wasn't trying to create any conflicts. And second, I didn't know who these prisoners were who came to my aid and I didn't want to involve them in any bullshit beefs. I left, to the great relief of everyone. As I was leaving, I decided to find out just what the situation surrounding the mess hall and the meals was. I had a number of questions. As I emptied my tray into the trashcans full of food that prisoners were forced to throw away, the main question was why was it so important to get everyone out of the mess hall in the shortest possible time? Why was the potential for violence so great over such a minor issue? The answer I would discover over the next few days was an odd rationale, but then again incarceration is often in conflict with what is rational.

What I was able to surmise is that the prison, and prisoners in general, was run on a loose basis because the control and enforcement machinery are concentrated in a few key areas. The two areas used most often to reinforce control over prisoners are the mess halls and the visiting rooms. Both are of great importance to prisoners and guards alike; the prisoners receive sustenance and human interaction in the mess hall and visiting room and the guards are able to demonstrate their force because the prisoners are the most vulnerable in those spaces. The mess hall is used just like Pavlov used food to train his dogs. The one area prisoners must appear in at least once a day is the mess hall. In this area they are made to file through and sit in seats appointed by any guards working mess hall duty. It is important for the authority of the guard force to be reinforced in the minds of prisoners on a daily basis, and the most effective training of animals and humans seems to occur through the use and control of food and its consumption. Friends are made and lost by what happens around the food trays.

All of the new guards (the "rookies") are trained in the mess hall. It's their first lesson in how to command and control prisoners. For their part, prisoners are hungry and simply want to get some food in their bellies. The regularity with which a prisoner is told where to sit and how long to stay creates a learned response that requires no thought. The prisoner becomes institutionalized and when that same prisoner is given a directive by a guard whether it is to walk, run, or eat, the response is automatic because the conditioning already occurred in the mess hall through the daily reinforcement of control and command. The visiting room offers the same type of conditioning stimuli, but the mess hall affords the guards the best opportunity to demonstrate force and thereby send a message to the population as a whole. Thus, the least amount of resistance to any guard's authority is met with immediate force, without compromise. The mess hall is a public forum and the lessons taught there are intended for the collective body of prisoners present at any given time. Since most prisoners are not trying to get involved in mass-riot types of situations, many will just watch an altercation develop—see the guard force come together and concentrate upon one or two prisoners who may be supporting a friend who is about to be taken away.

The ensuing situation almost always results in the prisoners receiving a ticket (the prison's way of charging prisoners for offenses real or imagined) for inciting a riot, which carries a heavy penalty, second only to assault on a guard. The lesson learned by most during these incidents is generally that a prisoner has no way to win in that kind of situation. Prisoners, for the most part, return to their housing area and maybe discuss what happened to "so and so" and how bad or mean Officer "so and so" was and how he is always doing something like this and causing trouble. The next time the general population sees the prisoner who had the conflict in the mess hall, it is months later. He looks bad after three months on lockup with few showers, half-rations of food, and daily combat situations, as well as little exercise and fewer visits. The likelihood is great that he is will get into a conflict and return to lockup in a week or less. Otherwise, he has changed his behavior or tact in dealing with the guard force. This tends to reinforce the lesson for the general population.

Prisoners tend to experience most of their conflicts around the food issue, and the most rebellious actions tend to come out of conflicts between prisoners around the quality of the food or the harassment received while getting or trying to eat it. The fact that a group of prisoners comes together and supports one another is a crime in and of itself. It is highly unusual for this to occur in the mess hall, but when it does, it is treated as an unforgivable offense, which is what I quickly found out on that very first night in the penitentiary. Once I returned to my cell, I sat down to write to a few friends, letting them know that I had been moved to the prison. As I sat on my bunk writing, a guard came to my door and stopped to look in for a minute or so. Naturally this attracted my attention, but before any interaction could take place he was gone. I thought about this a few seconds before continuing my letter, only to discover a commotion outside of my cell door.

This time the officer was accompanied by a captain and a lieutenant. The lieutenant says to the captain, "Here he is," and the Captain peeks into the cell and asks, "Where is this big bad two-hundred-fifty-pound tough guy? Not him!" and then continues, "Why are you giving my officers trouble?"

I attempted to explain that I didn't understand that someone could be rushed through supper and run out of the mess hall with half of the food uneaten. I wanted to know what the point was of giving people food that they were not allowed to consume, and why such a big deal was made over a guy attempting to finish his meal. It's not like I was trying to burn down the place or something! Anyway, he wasn't there to listen to me, or even for that matter to talk to me; he had merely been sent to warn me: Don't get involved with prisoners in the mess hall and don't start no trouble in "their" prison, and he was gone.

Over an hour later, a prisoner showed up and asked me if I was okay and brought me some magazines. He told me that the brothers said that if I needed anything to just let someone know that I wanted to see a Black Panther. Well, this was surely news to me. During the time that I had spent in the BPP in Baltimore, I was involved in all the organizing of the new chapters at one point or another, but I had no knowledge of any organizing going on in the Maryland Penitentiary. I thought, perhaps, that these were some fallen comrades that I was unaware of. Anyway, I looked forward to meeting the brothers the next day.

My first day out of the cell was a few days after the mess hall incident. I was sent to the hospital for a physical check-up. I was in the waiting room when the brother in charge of the Panthers came in and identified himself as the Field Marshal. With him were two of his lieutenants and a rank-and-file member. This brother had been dealing with the South Baltimore branch of the Panthers; he impressed me as well-read and informed on the party and its programs. One look at this brother with his big red bush and dark glasses, his field jacket and boots and took me back to the days in Oakland and the party convention. I talked to these brothers for the hours I spent down at the hospital waiting for the physical. I was sorry to find out after really talking to them that they were more show and reaction than knowledge and action. I think I decided at that point not to get involved with them. I believed that they were stand-up brothers, but they demonstrated little to no discipline and lacked organizational skills and structure. However, they had already decided that I was the new, though unofficial, leader and therefore I would take charge.

Well, of course this wasn't in my program at all. First, I was determined not to work to reform a criminal system that was oppressing my people, and second, my feelings were that I didn't want to spend a whole lot of time fucking around with a bunch of prison conditions and minor problems that ignored the real issues or solutions to the larger issue of oppression. I was concerned with the issues that were affecting our survival; the conditions that our communities were being subjected to; the repression and oppression that the political and economic arrangement in America was creating to our continued disadvantage; the massive killings of our youth and the developing drug problem in our neighborhoods; the hungry children in our streets and the massive unemployment among our men. These were the kinds of things that concerned me at that time on the national level. The international situation in relation to Vietnam, Africa, and South America held what remained of my attention.

I really had no time for the food conditions of the penitentiary or the fact that the guards were real pigs. It was what I expected to be a part of the program in prison. After all, our brother George Jackson was going through hell out in California. This didn't mean that I was completely insensitive to the plight of the prisoners there; rather, I didn't think that organizing under these conditions would really have any kind of an impact on the prisoners or the conditions. At the time, I just couldn't see how organizing inside of a prison would benefit black people in general. I had no understanding of how the growth of the prison industrial complex would affect African-descended and Latino communities. Nor was I cognizant of the fact that the growth coincided with the struggle for self-determination and Black Power that many of us in the Black Panther Party had been committed to.

It was only after spending some time with a number of these brothers that I realized that a good many of them were really very serious and were trying to gain an understanding of the forces and factors that were having such dire impact on black people in particular, but also oppressed people in general. I was suddenly faced with the fact that I needed to re-examine my position. After some soul searching, I asked myself if I should or really could allow these brothers to continue to struggle and seek knowledge on their own. The answer was easy; I knew that I could aid in their growth and development if I spent some time with them. After all, the key duty of any real activist is to educate as many people as possible to the conditions or positions of the movement and the struggle. Here was a group of really raw brothers crying out to be molded and mentored for the benefit of the masses. I was committed to change, and if I could help a number of these brothers raise their consciousness and take a position like mine for the good of the community then I would do it.

And so, within the first few weeks of my confinement, I was already engaged in organizing a number of activities. Since I had been doing this kind of work on the streets it had become second nature, and so it wasn't hard to get the ball rolling inside. Prison has always been a fertile ground for organizing. There is always a highly motivated segment, however small, among the population, because prisoners live under the most oppressive conditions that one can imagine. Outside, in the community at large, it could be more difficult to motivate people. Community organizers are always faced with a number of distractions: the amount of time needed to deal with employment and travel between home and the office; the time needed to maintain a reasonable social life or partnership of some type; other distractions, like family-related situations or the showdown at the Civic Center. Prisoners have none of these distractions.

In prison, the job is right there in the compound and the travel time is nil. The family and social situation is limited, at best, to writing letters at night or receiving occasional visits from friends and family. No one moves away or goes to concerts. The problem of burnout exists for prisoners, but there is sometimes a stronger peer group and this helps to support and reinforce the values of the group. The motivation for being involved might be any number of things, but the prevalent one among the population is usually the basic living conditions and general treatment of prisoners at the hands of the guards. So there was a captive audience, so to speak, in the penitentiary; the people being organized were always available morning, noon, and night and the motivation for involvement was continuously reinforced by the prison administration itself. It seemed like the ideal situation for an organizer, but I had to wonder why my hair was turning gray. This being my first experience with imprisonment, I was somewhat naïve. I would soon find out that the potential for conflict was a constant and ever-present danger—one that was encouraged by various elements within the guard force.

The Maryland Penitentiary occupied two city blocks in the black community of East Baltimore. The city's population was about 750,000 people at that time. The prison housed 1,300 men from all over the state, but the majority of its population was from Baltimore City itself. There was not one day that went by without some act of violence occurring in the prison. This small area must have had the highest crime rate in the city. The internal violence was tolerated and often encouraged by the administration in order to maintain control of the men within the structure's confines. One group would frequently be pitted against another in what amounted to an orgy of violent frustration; the resultant aggression was transferred from guards to other prisoners. This made it twice as hard to organize, since every conflict could remove a number of brothers from the general population area for fifteen to 90 days at a time. These brothers would go on lockup mad, and once there they would become even more hostile than before.

This sometimes trumped the political education and training that we were giving the men, because it was likely just beginning to have some impact on their behavior. The hostility and violence that they were immediately subjected to put them back on the defensive, even just for reasons of survival. Whether on the street or within the prison environment, combat was the resolution to most problems for these cats. It was the course of action most often taken by the majority of the lockup population and those guarding them. Nevertheless, organizing within the prison was a necessity and it became something that many brothers wanted to do beyond anything else, so it was done. There were about forty or fifty brothers who were the actual members of the Black Panther Party chapter in the prison and they had about one hundred supporters. Initially the lack of discipline from the rank-and-file members would be a barrier to organizing because of both the lack of political consciousness and an organized structure, but we would soon work together to overcome these limitations.

The first thing we did was to form collective units in each housing area and assign officers to supervise the training and other activities. We created a set of policies that all members had to adhere to and made political education and physical education mandatory. We then formed a number of action committees to deal with various needs such as communications and information, security, and education. It seemed that in addition to the daily violence occurring within the prison, there was at least one major incident involving the guards every few months. The first one that I witnessed started in the yard and the reason was unclear. All I remember is that prisoners started to gather in the yard on one end and guards on the other. By the time both groups arrived at the meeting point the situation was volatile.

On the prisoners' side there were at least two hundred men with sticks, pipes, and other assorted weapons of gang warfare. On the other side there were about twenty-five to thirty rank-and-file guards with shields and riot sticks. They stood between the prisoners and the only exit out of the yard barring at least two hundred other prisoners who were not involved in the standoff from leaving the site of conflict. Far beyond them was another line of guards. These were mainly the supervisors, lieutenants, and captains, and they were armed with rifles and shotguns. Up until that time I believe it was against the law to bring deadly weapons into the actual prison yard. They must have recently gotten the law changed because the older prisoners were just as surprised as the newer ones.

Up in the windows overlooking the yard were two riflemen with weapons poised to take the life of anyone who stepped too far out of line. I was taking the whole situation in carefully because it looked like there was going to be a riot—this was some time before the uprising at Attica. One of the things that made the situation worse was the fact that, for the past three weeks or so, there had been a number of warning signs indicating that there would be trouble if the guards did not let up on the repression and abuse that they had wrought on the men. Incident after incident had occurred and each brought with it more complaints from old and young prisoners alike. This point is important, because as a rule older prisoners don't involve themselves in general situations. If it did not personally involve them or their close friends, the administration never heard a word from them. Over the past few weeks this had changed; a wide range of prisoners were suddenly beefing about the conditions and treatment that they were being subjected to.

Everyone agreed that the living conditions were getting worse and the officers more abusive—if, in an environment where the term "nigger" was used regularly by the guards, such a thing was possible. It felt as if many of the guards had conspired to create the conditions that would lead to a riot in order to obtain greater control through a total lockdown and ever-increasing repression. This would mean that all the prisoners were locked in their cell twenty-four hours a day. This was perhaps a guard's daily fantasy: nothing to do all day but walk by a cell once an hour. The entire prison would become a lockup unit and there would be few exceptions regarding movement among the prisoners; only a select few men would be allowed to move about, and only because they held essential jobs like food-handling and clean-up. Other exceptions would be the typists and record-keepers who ran the prison for the guards.

During a general lockdown there would be no showers, no exercise walks, very little medical treatment, and very few visits. The prison could remain like this for as little as one day to as long as one or two years, depending on the situation that caused the lockdown. So that day out in the yard, everyone knew that the situation had come to a head. There were going to be some deaths and injuries on both sides. The odds were not in favor of the prisoners since they lacked the firepower of the guards and they would surely suffer the consequences for the uprising. However, the prisoners were poised to bring the odds down, and with so much at stake both sides faced off and stared one another down. A few terse words passed between the two groups but no physical contact had been made. The faces of the men on both sides reflected their goals, some wanted to get it over with and others wanted to stop it, yet each side knew there was a need to resolve this situation before it was too late.

The prisoners demanded a meeting with the warden to discuss the conditions and treatment that they were subjected to, including the increased harassment. The guards, on the other hand, continued to demand that the prisoners clear the yard, which was an unreasonable if not impossible demand since their ranks were blocking the only exit out of the yard. This resulted in an obvious stalemate because some of the prisoners did not want to leave the yard and others couldn't even if they wanted to. The guards could not go back inside and they weren't going to let us go between them or behind them. The demands and threats continued on both sides, but it was clear that this situation still had time to be resolved without bloodshed. It was at this point that something happened that was totally unexpected by both the guards and the prisoners.

One of the black guards pulled off his helmet and crossed over to our side. Just as suddenly, another joined us. Soon there were half a dozen black guards standing among the ranks of the prisoners. They demanded that the warden come hear our grievances. These men told us to be cool, assuring us all that they would stand with us even if it meant putting their jobs on the line because they wanted to avoid bloodshed on both sides. Then the other guards backed off because they could not justify attacking us with their own men standing safely within our midst. It was plain to see that we had some purpose behind our demands to speak with the warden, and that we were not just bent on rioting for the hell of it. Finally, the officials agreed that a small group of us could meet with the warden to address the issues that were continuously being raised by the crowd.

All of the prisoners were instructed to return to our respective housing areas. From among us, a group was selected to meet with the administration and the rest of the prisoners filed through a gauntlet of guards back to their cells. A meeting was held with the warden and he agreed to look into the situation and correct anything that seemed wrong. The conditions in the yard got a little better and the level of harassment dropped significantly for a while, but gradually the same abuses started to occur again. Three months later it was as if nothing had ever changed; in fact, as time went on, things got even worse. It appeared that the guards were trying to make the point that things don't get better by rebelling and, at the same time, the population was saying, "Well, the next time we will just take it all the way." The mood remained ugly and tense.

Chapter Seven

After George

August 21, 1971 found me and a number of my comrades on lockup in the segregation unit. During the early part of my imprisonment, lockup was a frequent experience for me. Most of the time, I ended up there as a result of my organizing, but it was also a general principle situation: the administration kept me there because they could, and because this would prevent the organizing. The south wing of the penitentiary housed the punishment unit and it held up to four hundred prisoners locked in their cells for twenty-three and a half hours every day. We spent the other thirty minutes in the shower or getting exercise; the activities alternated every day. Many of us had radios but kept them hidden during the day shift, between eight in the morning and four in the afternoon. We didn't find out about George Jackson's death until that evening when we pulled our radios out. This sad news quickly passed through the entire unit, and soon the only sound heard was the rumble of the low voices of the comrades asking for updates, and the almost inaudible noise caused by suppressing a scream for too long. This was the sound of three hundred years of oppression. Like those whistles that are audible only to the animal ear, this sound is only for the keen ears of the oppressed. So, the men swallowed their rage, literally choking it back down, but like all angry emotion, it would eventually inhabit many of the prisoners like an evil spirit bent on possession.

I certainly had no illusions about imprisonment; it had always been clear to me that the comrades in prison were the easiest to attack. While

I was personally shocked, I was well aware of the fate that would befall anyone who rebelled against the police state. That night, we held an observance for the death of Comrade George marked by three minutes of silence and a discussion of his life and work. We talked about his death, and many of us were concerned about how the loss of such a significant leader would affect the prison movement. I felt that his death signaled the beginning of the end for the movement. Drugs would soon sate the appetite of the rebellious prisoner. Many of the former rebels would themselves become peddlers of the poison, assisting the government in its genocidal plan for a few coins. Like modern day Judases, they would betray the people over and over again. Looking back, these were extremely hard times and things were looking bad, so the substance abuse helped prisoners to escape that reality, as well as their past realities.

We continued our work while on lockup with a variety of activities. There were education classes three nights a week, and daily physical training. We also supplied basic necessities such as toiletries for men who were in need, and kept a small library of books that floated among prisoners. These activities were all that we felt we could safely do under the current conditions. Yet it was still not enough because the drug use seemed to increase and soon we had to address the issue in our education classes. This resulted in a campaign to help brothers get off the drugs. Initially the effort was very successful; one by one, the brothers were declaring to the lockup population that they were no longer using or seeking drugs. Living in lockup was like living in an open community so it was easy to determine if someone was in fact still using. Everyone knew everyone else's business and enough men were involved in the campaign to provide a wide network of support and ensure that those men who were using had a non-user nearby.

Just when we thought that everything was going well, things took a tragic turn. A brother hung himself, and then the next day another brother did the same; both of them had given up drugs. It was then that we made a decision to suspend the campaign, but it would be too late for yet another brother. This death touched my soul. It shook me at the very core, and I must admit it even scared me because it was such a shock. A few days after we suspended the campaign, a brother who was housed two cells down the tier from me asked if he could borrow my *Little Red Book*. After our nightly political discussions, the comrades would often "research" the topics, and so this brother said he wanted to look up something that we had covered in the last class. At the time, we were all out of our cells for exercise: a thirty-minute walk on the tier. Lunch was served soon after we were locked back into our cells, and I received my meal with the same lack of enthusiasm that I would always feel toward prison food. The prisoners who were passing the food out moved on to the next cell and then on to the next, when they abruptly dropped everything and ran to the end of the tier to summon a guard.

I watched as the guard rushed to the cell while calling for help, but it was too late. The same brother who had only moments ago been contemplating last night's political education class had hung himself. I was dumbstruck because he had seemed as if everything was normal. Later, when I looked at that *Little Red Book*, I found myself asking if I might have missed something when we talked. Had there been a clue or the least little inkling that he was suicidal? At that point, I decided that we would never take away anyone's crutch without first filling that void with something to sustain the individual. While education is good, in no way does it mask the pain that the drugs have been covering up. If anything, the education was opening many of these men's eyes to the suffering that black people had experienced, and this, coupled with imprisonment itself, was equivalent to opening a vein.

It was not long after I arrived at the penitentiary that I began smoking, a habit I would struggle with for many years to come. One day, I was summoned by a group of brothers who had taken members of the prison laundry staff as hostages. These men said they were tired of being exploited. They were barely able to purchase cigarettes with the money that they were making in the prison laundry and the price had recently gone up. In protest they staged a non-violent take over of the wing where the laundry was and I was called on to negotiate with the guards. I needed a smoke; the urge was new, but real. It became a habit that would plague me, because I had never experienced a dependence on any substance and I would always feel that my smoking was a weakness.

There was a lot of organizing going on across the nation in almost every community. Prisons around the country were organizing themselves based on the strong trends coming out of California and New York. The men at Attica had just made their grievances known to the public via outside networks. Massive organizing was going on there and at most of

California's prisons. In New York, organizers were working to get as many people involved in the movement for human rights as possible. Their slogan was "we are men not animals," while on the other coast the type of organizing was very selective and often connected to a specific political ideology as in the case of the Black Guerrilla Family, a group that originally shared ties to the Black Panther Party through Comrade George. The situation for the many comrades in the California penal system was one of sheer survival.

Since we had much in common with the comrades in California and New York, we decided to do both types of organizing. There would be some selective organizing to develop a cadre, and some mass organizing around general prison issues to get more people involved. Thus, we decided upon a vehicle that would allow us room to do both; we would form the United Prisoners Labor Union. Upon doing some research, we found that the law permitted us to form a union, since technically we worked for the state in a collective manner. We began the basic tasks that needed completion before we could officially become a union. First, it was necessary to write up a charter and some bylaws covering the full range of union benefits and responsibilities. Next, we had to sign up one third of the work force (i.e. population), which totaled about five hundred prisoners. Then, we had to find an outside union that would accept us; SEIU 1199E had begun to work with us, and so they agreed to accept us.

We were also required to form an outside advisory board to coordinate between us, the prison administration, and the parent organization. And finally, we had to hold an open election in the workplace to make sure that there were enough prisoners desiring a union. So many of us spent weeks reading and studying other unions' bylaws and agreements, and after what seemed like too many meetings, we produced a finished copy of our union charter and bylaws. While this had been going on, some members had been assigned to do outreach. This included working the yard and talking to the general population about the need for a union, as well as describing the process that was necessary to establish one. They also had to sign up as many people as possible so that we would meet the required numbers.

This job was done by all of us at some point in the process. It was perhaps the hardest part of the whole program because the administration was pushing a counter-union movement. This agenda was being carried out by members of one of the new youth gangs that had formed within the prison population, and was beginning to grow fast. The New Family, as it was called, claimed to not only be the new wave in the prison population but also the future gangsters of Baltimore. This group was led by a small clique of tough guys and "fuck boys" (members of the prison bisexual culture) who not only worked with the administration, but also had the ear of the youth population, especially newly arrived youth looking for a protection hookup. This group had no politics to speak of, but the leaders viewed themselves as godfathers helping the government against communist elements that were misleading the population.

This group was working day and night to oppose the union and our organizing efforts. They kept telling the population that this was a communist thing and un-American. They were capitalists and therefore believed in "free enterprise" which they were willing to work for, even if it meant working for the administration. Many was the time that one of our organizers would be working with a group of prisoners, explaining the charter, going over the different points and answering questions they might have, when along would come one or two New Family members to disrupt things. They would attempt to distract everyone by sparking a debate on any number of issues. Where was the money coming from to pay minimum wages and who was going to pay the union officials, they would ask, and then suggest that this effort would simply get the state mad at us and result in the authorities pulling all the workshops out of the penitentiary and giving them to another prison in the state without a union. So on and so on.

At other times, our organizers would find themselves confronted by guards who would query them about what they were doing, or ask more threatening questions about what they had in their pockets. This would almost always lead to a search or shakedown, and in some cases heated words would be exchanged and our organizer would end up on lockup with a bum rap.

Yet in spite of all the efforts to stop the union organizing, we signed up over five hundred men with a lot of serious work by many brothers in the yard. At the same time that we were enjoying this success, two other things were occurring. One was the union's executive board accepting us officially and involving itself in giving us support by contacting the prison officials on our behalf. This particular union was a good choice to work with because of its history. It had been engaged in a struggle to organize the hospital workers in Baltimore, and the fact that this had been an ongoing battle for two years made it a real tough job. We knew that unionizing the prison would also prove difficult. 1199E also happened to be the union that Dr. Martin Luther King had been working with before his assassination in Memphis, Tennessee; they were organizing the sanitation workers.

And, finally, this union had positive leadership and a good organizer in Fred Punch, who was the president at that time. He was bold and outspoken when it came to expressing the concerns and interests of the people he was working with. We needed that kind of positive and progressive support and thought we could get it from 1199E. Once we had made contact with them and developed a common platform that we could work with collectively, we were able to garner enough support from the population to win the vote. Another group had simultaneously been working to develop an outside advisory board. We contacted a number of community leaders and explained what we were trying to do to better our conditions at the penitentiary, and a number of them agreed to act as members of an advisory board, including radio personality Kitty Broady, Parren Mitchell who would later become a Maryland Congressman, Paul Coates, a comrade from the Black Panther Party and the owner of Black Classic Press, and others. This ad hoc advisory board contacted the officials at the penitentiary and arranged meetings between all of the parties.

The organizing that was happening in the prison yard was going so well we decided to downgrade the amount of union activities there and re-direct our attention toward the development of committees that would carry out the union programs and policies once we won acceptance. As I look back, these were wild and foolish days because even though we expected to be attacked, we did not expect the lengths to which the administration would go to put an end to the organizing. Since we were working within legal boundaries, we figured that any attack on us would clearly be seen as an attack. It never occurred to us that they would frame us to make it stick. We were doing serious organizing and doing it aboveground and legally. The level of success was surprising even to us. We had no idea that the vast majority of the prisoners wanted something like this so badly that they were ready to meet any crisis or work around any problems. The general population worked hard at building a union despite the interference of the youth gangs. The prisoners who held jobs and positions that couldn't be linked to the union organizing efforts for fear of retaliation from the administration willingly did everything that we needed done secretly. The support of these men was extremely important to the development of the union. Some of the work they did was more serious than the work that some of the members did because they supplied information about the prison's finances, specifically the fact that prisoners were receiving what amounted to pennies while they produced millions in profit for the prison industry.

For every two people who signed up, there was at least one other prisoner who actively supported the union without joining. We had a wide range of members and supporters, from the very old to the very youngest prisoners, who were developing a consciousness and awareness of the need for change. The whole population was full of positive energy and in high spirits because there was real hope for change at last. Even many of the prisoners who we had labeled as "toms" openly broke with the administration over the issue of the union. Needless to say, while all this was going on, the administration was planning their counterattack to disrupt our organizing efforts and union activities. Minor incidents began to occur, and it looked as if they would soon grow into a major situation.

We found ourselves acting as union marshals—or more precisely as peacekeepers—so that the general population would not be tricked into engaging in negative activities that might be blamed on the union organizing efforts, or that might affect the official establishment of the union. Most of the troubleshooting was done on the spot, between individual prisoners and guards who had some sort of personal beef. It became very clear right from the start that the guards were turning up the pressure on the entire population and the incidents were not at all random. The selection of specific prisoners for harassment made it clear that this was an organized effort by the guards. The prisoners stopped and searched most frequently were those who were all too likely to become violent. This harassment was continual during this period.

The very fact that imprisonment involves so many rules that it is difficult not to be in violation of some rule at any given time lent itself to this harassment. The guards rarely enforce the very petty rules and regulations, like those that define limits on what a prisoner may have in his cell at any given time—such as five pens or pencils, or twenty stamps. There are other vague rules concerning how a prisoner looks at a guard, be it lustful or hostile—this is called "reckless eyeballing," and the interpretation of your gaze is left to the individual guard. To raise one's voice during a disagreement with a guard could result in a charge. The very space in which a prisoner plants his feet might place him in violation of a rule. One guard could see the prisoner's feet six inches over a yellow line and determine that he is out of bounds, another guard might consider it an escape attempt, yet another may simply tell the prisoner to move on. Because the enforcement of these rules is at the whim of the individual guard, things can go south quickly if the parties involved have a hostile relationship, or if the administration wants to turn up the heat on the population.

We had to keep talking to the prisoners subject to the most harassment, and while most of them really supported the union, their tempers tended to get out of hand sometimes. The fact that they supported the union and could see that the administration was looking for a major incident to derail the union made these brothers hang in there and sometimes even accept the harassment with a smile. The prison officials soon realized that there was so much support for the union that the population was policing itself. Any man starting trouble would get pulled up by another prisoner and stopped, or taken away and isolated, depending on the nature of his response to the others prisoners. Most prisoners would realize what was happening once someone stopped them for a second and pointed it out. They would smile and walk away from the situation on their own and, because of this self-control and discipline in the general population, we thought we had the situation under control. We were wrong about that. Within a few days of the failed harassment attempts, the key leaders of the union were placed on lockup one night in a midnight raid on the housing areas.

At the next level of attack, we found ourselves charged with illegal organizing of an unauthorized organization. All thirty-nine of the union's leaders were removed from the general population, leaving the committee chairman with over five hundred angry and leaderless members. We had agreed beforehand to counsel calmness and control if something like a mass arrest took place. That night, before leaving the housing units, we reinforced this concept with all the secondary leadership we could find. We told them to make sure that everyone was cool and not to allow this massive lockup to distract them from the real issue: the need for the union. It was our belief that, once we succeeded in our task, this type of repressive behavior on the part of the officials would no longer be easy to carry out.

Placed on lockup yet again, I waited along with everyone else to see what the morrow would bring. Collectively, we discussed our hope that the chairman would be able to control the situation. I had a cell in front of one of the windows that allowed me to see out into the yard. I watched the prisoners file out in the yard to go to breakfast and then on to work. I knew then that response would slowly develop throughout the day among the population, since they had talked from cell to cell in the hours after we were locked up. They were milling around and asking questions about what should really be done now. I could see some of the more hot-headed members and a few outsiders demanding that something happen to show the administration that they could not keep doing this to us. The political education classes paid off here, because the comrades managed the situation beautifully, gaining control so that there was not a single incident.

Over the next few days, the outside executive support worked on meeting with the commissioner of corrections and the prison administration about the mass lockup of our leadership. At this point, the administration moved into phase two of their attack on us. In the middle of the night, we were all sitting at our doors on lockup, proudly talking about the future of the union, and how the population was standing firm. Word came in from one of the runners that there was an incident going down in the west wing. A number of prisoners had climbed up into the windows. The upper-level windows were at least seventy-five feet high, and the flats were made of concrete, so if someone fell from that height it was likely to be serious, if not fatal. Those of us on lockup had no idea about what caused the incident, or who was involved in it, but the situation remained at a stalemate for several hours.

Apparently, it had all started around 9 or 10PM that evening and it was not until about 2 or 3AM when the men came down from the windows. The guards started bringing the men over to lockup and this was the first chance we got to see who they were. Right from the beginning it looked all wrong. The majority of these men were known drug addicts and the others were mostly likely users as well. Why in the world would drug addicts be doing something as rebellious as refusing to lock-in and going up into the windows, when they had never before been involved in any protest or any other proactive activities? And, on top of that, most of these drug addicts were known to us as informers for the administration. The fact that there was not one union member or progressive individual among them let us know right away that this was another effort to undermine our union-building.

The next day the entire institution was locked down and the window incident was blamed on the union organizers. The prison administration held a press conference during which they claimed that the union was responsible for this rebellious act, that it was a reaction to the mass arrest of the illegal organizers. In essence, they said that we were simply bad elements in the prison trying to stir up trouble. To add insult to injury, they also went so far as to claim that the Advisory Board members had been misled by us, and didn't realize what they were doing by encouraging us in this destructive behavior. They would have to be protected from us since they did not understand the mentality of prisoners. The prison administration informed Advisory Board members that they could no longer meet with us. In addition, the members were prohibited from doing any union organizing within the Department of Corrections or the penitentiary. The next day the entire union leadership received sixty to ninety days on lockup for organizing the union.

The prison itself remained locked down for another full week to let the general population know that more would be coming if the union kept growing. Some people received transfers to other institutions as disciplinary measures. The resulting news story referred to the situation as "the human fly incident," and completely eclipsed the truth. The papers carried the story from the administration's viewpoint: they made the union look like a gang of troublemakers and our community supporters seem like uninformed liberals who had unknowingly encouraged this behavior. The union backed out of their commitment to us, and with our outside supporters barred from the institution and the internal leadership of the union locked up, the union drive in the penitentiary just died. When the prison opened back up a week later, all union activities were banned and all union and lecture materials was declared illegal by the officials, who gave orders to arrest anyone caught with them. The administration had used the human flies to kill off the union … but the flies would be back soon enough to haunt the administration.

Chapter Eight

Fly on the Wall

Several weeks later, while we were still on lockup, a lone prisoner was demanding medical treatment for some problem he had. It was four days before the guards decided to take him to the hospital, and once there, he never even got to see the doctor. The doctor, he was told, was on call, but he would only be summoned for emergencies, and normal medical problems would have to be handled by the nurse. Well, this prisoner only got to see the nurse and he was not happy when he returned to the lockup area. He requested a talk with the supervisor about his problem, but his request was refused, and so, out of the frustration more than anything else, he broke away from the guards and climbed up into the windows. At first no one understood what was going on because the situation was happening on the other side of the lockup so most guards and prisoners assumed it was some kind of fight. All we could hear were shouts coming from the other side.

"That's right ... fuck them punks ... go on with it," and "...be careful brother ...."

It would be a few minutes before the guards who went running around to that side looking for a confrontation became aware that a human fly was back. Soon, as was always the case with such an incident, a mob of officials came to the lockup area to talk to this prisoner. It never failed: if a prisoner needed to talk to a supervisor, they were always too busy, but as soon as the prisoner took some type of action, there were more "officials" on the scene than one might see in a year. Now, all of a sudden, they all

Just like WMD

wanted to know what the problem was, and why no one had informed them about this medical situation. Would the brother please come down so they could take care of the situation and get him to the doctor right away? In fact, they said, the doctor was on his way in right at that moment. Well, this brother did not seem to buy it, and it turned out that he had requested to see a supervisor a number of times before, and each time he had gotten the runaround. They had given in and taken him to the hospital finally just to keep him quiet, but it was to no avail.

Almost every official in the prison was now standing around on the flats trying to convince the brother that they all were concerned about his medical problems, but he didn't want to talk to them about it any more; the brother now wanted to talk to the news media. He informed them that he was not coming down until he could talk to the press. Since he was in the windows facing the street outside of the prison, people passing along Forrest Street could see and hear him. The officials did not want to shoot him out of the window in front of the public, so they were at a loss as to what to do to deal with him. They had brought in mattresses and stun guns to shoot him down, but the people outside were already talking to him. They asked him what his name was, and some folks promised to call the media.

The administrators inside the prison could not talk him out of the window, and it was clear that they had no intention of meeting his demand to hold a press conference about the medical treatment of the prisoners. The situation reached a stalemate, and then turned into a standoff, with the prison officials withdrawing to plan another course of action. The brother had the run of the south wing area since he could cross over to the other side by climbing over the back shower area. He travelled from level to level by climbing up and down the grilles in front of our cells. This gave him direct access to each prisoner on the lockup section with the exception of the prisoners on the flats because it was too risky to go down on the ground level. This amounted to contact with well over two hundred prisoners and together they fed him and gave him warm clothes along with a long list of grievances to give to the press on their behalf.

The next day, two more prisoners joined him up in the windows after returning from the visiting room. They climbed up in the windows to great applause, and soon another prisoner who was returning from the Adjustment Team hearing room, where he had received more time on lockup, joined the others in the window. Later that night, another prisoner had his attempt to join the men thwarted. However, the next day brought a number tries from more prisoners and two of these men were successful, though most were stopped by the guards. Nevertheless, the human fly situation was growing too fast for the officials to keep up with it. The news media turned out to cover the happenings, but the prison officials prevented reporters from speaking to the prisoners. The media was honoring an unwritten agreement—they never reported incidents inside the prison unless prison officials okayed it. ✶ *Wow*

Despite the administration's best efforts to prevent coverage of the situation, people outside were taking an interest in what was happening inside the prison. They wanted to know what could have caused this kind of behavior. Prisoners told visitors coming into the visiting room about the grievances that were, by then, the collective demands of the "Flies," who were now representatives for the entire lockup section. This had moved from an incident involving a single individual to a general protest of the living conditions in the lockup section. The Flies had been talking to anyone who would stop and listen on the street below the prison windows. The nine hundred block of Forrest Street was an open area that ran in front of the prison, and it had a good deal of traffic throughout the day and a nominal amount at night. In fact, this street served as a shortcut from downtown Baltimore to the nearby black community. Many people coming from work or shopping trips downtown would pass through this street. Visitors to the prison would also come down this street, as well as employees working in the surrounding administrative complex.

Many of these people were stopping to talk to the prisoners in the windows, trying to find out what was going on. Soon, there were people who were coming by just to talk to the prisoners. The officials decided they could not allow the number of Flies to increase, so they ordered the guards to handcuff anyone who was out of their cell for any reason. All prisoners now had to be escorted by three guards at all times. This made for an extremely difficult situation since only four or five guards were normally stationed in the south wing at any given time. This meant that if someone went on visit, it could be almost two hours late because of the lack of manpower. The fly group stopped growing, but visitors began to complain about the amount of time they had to spend waiting for prisoners in the visiting area.

The plan was working well for the prisoners on lockup—it's impossible to climb into the windows with handcuffs on. But the officials overlooked something: the whole lockup unit was staffed by prisoners who did all of the labor. They passed out the food and the sheets, cleaned the floors, and packed and moved the property of those prisoners on lockup. They also did paperwork, and ordered supplies. All of these prisoners had friends on lockup, or they had been locked up themselves at some point in the past. Those who had worked in the south wing lockup unit the longest had seen a lot of abuse and mistreatment of prisoners behind the doors. Some of the guards had singled out different prisoners to be harassed and kept in the unit by continuing to give them new charges and new sentences.

The prisoners working there would see all this and sometimes they would carry news and information out to the general population to "contact so and so's people because he just got beat up by the pigs," or let us know that someone else didn't receive any treatment for this or that ailment. Other times they would join in the protest about this or that problem that the men behind the door might have, and in real serious cases they would even go to the supervisor about the conditions. There have even been times when the workers have stood up for a prisoner who was out by himself and under the threat of attack by the guards while in handcuffs and unable to defend himself. The workers would stand with him until the guards put him back into the cell. All too often, specific prisoners the guards wanted to beat would be brought out late at night, and jumped on, and thrown into the hole or isolation unit away from everyone else. It would be days sometimes before anyone saw them or knew if they were okay. They might need treatment for something broken or a deep cut or anything else, but no help was forthcoming to these brothers. And all the workers knew this could be their fate at any time in the future.

It was not unusual for prisoners brought from the population to be attacked in the isolation area before being placed in the lockup cell. The workers would know someone was in the hole and being beaten, but they frequently couldn't find out who it was for hours, or sometimes even days. This was also hard on them, and they suppressed a lot of anger against the guards while working in that area. Well, given all of that, it's not surprising that once the prisoners in the cells were stopped from joining the "Flies" in the windows by the handcuff order, the workers started to join. Two of them climbed into the window before the rest were locked up in an area away from the windows. Eventually, seven prisoners were climbing all over the housing unit windows, and the press was camped out in the street with a number of supporters who had also camped outside the windows to see that nothing happened to their friends and family members inside the prison.

The Black Panthers, local black church groups, and other progressive groups and concerned citizens had actually set up a "squatters" camp outside the south wing, and they were refusing to leave. They vowed to stay there until the situation inside was resolved. The combined support of so many different groups and the daily presence of the local media put real pressure on the prison officials, who finally agreed to resolve the situation. They allowed a press conference, and the "Human Flies" were interviewed and presented their list of grievances. Community leaders were called on to ensure the men's safety, and to see that they were not attacked later. However, after the press attention dwindled, and some weeks after a few minor changes occurred, the situation slipped right back to the same old abusive and repressive relations between guards and prisoners.

For a few short weeks, prisoners had used the same tactics against the administration that they had used to break our union drive; their own ghosts were now haunting them. The support that we received from grassroots members of the Baltimore community during the union drive and the second "Human Fly" incident helped to change the way many prisoners thought about the community outside the prison and its people. Suddenly there was interest in what was going on in the community, and the one thing that stood out was the lack of information prisoners had about the community at large. There were four television sets for the whole population of over seventeen-hundred prisoners. A few prisoners ordered the daily newspapers, but most men had to rely on the local radio station for news and information about what was happening outside. In many cases, the news coming from the local black radio stations was no news at all. At best, there was thirty to sixty seconds of junk news that had little or no real relevance to the daily situation and struggle in the black community. The men would find themselves passing around rumors and misinformation in an effort to keep up with what was happening.

Several of us decided that we could have an impact on the situation if we had our own newspaper. Since it was impossible for us to simply start producing a newspaper immediately, we settled for a one-page newsletter that covered weekly news and events. The Maryland Penitentiary Inter-Communal Survival Collective put this newsletter out, working from a cell in our housing area. The issues of the local papers and the underground papers we managed to acquire were perused and items we thought were of the most interest for the prison population would be extracted from them and encapsulated so that we could get as many news items as possible on that single page. This paper would be mimeographed and sent to each housing area in bundles. This caused problems almost right away because we could see from reading all the newspapers available to us that there were big differences in the political and social perspectives. Also problematic was the fact that some black community newspapers were allowed to come into the prison while others were classified as too radical or a threat to the security of the institution—an interesting fact in and of itself.

The Black Muslim newspaper *Muhammad Speaks* would come into the prison by the hundreds. The administration allowed it to be sold openly in the yard and anywhere else, but banned the black leftist papers. *The Black Panther* had to be smuggled into the prison and secretly passed from hand to hand. Any person caught with a copy would go on lockup for a long time. Once you put the two papers together you could see right away the many differences between them. Both papers covered non-political issues in much the same manner and light; the real difference came into play when the issues were about the economy, race, or international affairs. *Muhammad Speaks* always assumed pro-capitalist positions whether the story was about Africa or black folks in the US. Many of us felt that this paper seemed to be blaming the black community for economic injustice; we thought they were blaming the victim.

The editors and writers at *Muhammad Speaks* often filtered the issues of race and racism through the framework of their religious beliefs. The old story of the white man as the devil, and the black race as the chosen people was not enough to help folks develop a real analysis of the issues they were facing. The stories that covered the global situation had a slant from one of two possible perspectives: the economic structure of the country involved or the religion of the country involved. If the country was a capitalist nation or it was Islamic, it could do no wrong. *Muhammad Speaks* presented the leaders of these countries as the world's greatest men. A case in point was their portrayal of Uganda's leader, Idi Amin. The reports coming through most news media suggested that serious troubles were developing in Uganda, but *Muhammad Speaks* depicted the situation quite differently. According to the paper, the stories that revealed Amin to be a despot were all lies; Amin was, in fact, the greatest thing that had every happened to Uganda, and to the entire black race, and the African leaders in the surrounding countries who denounced Amin were the ones who deserved scorn.

The Black Panther, on the other hand, dealt with stories concerning the economy from a class perspective and with a left-wing political outlook. The paper blamed the ruling class and the capitalist structure of the government for the conditions that affected the poor and black communities of the world. *The Black Panther* also addressed the issue of race differently: all the people of the world were equally a part of the human family with a small minority responsible for most of the world's problems. The paper asserted that there was a continual struggle between the different classes of each society and racism was a tool used to divide us to keep us weak in our struggle against the ruling class. On most every page, the stories addressed the fact that black people and poor people needed to fight against racism and work with all people engaged in struggle to gain our freedom. From the perspective of the prison administration, these notions were dangerous to the population.

In *The Black Panther*, the international class struggle was always up front. Often, the same event or situation would be covered by both papers, in wildly different ways. The death of George Jackson was a story that affected the black liberation movement on the national level, while *Time Magazine*'s man of the year award to the president of Egypt, Anwar Sadat, had international impact for black and African communities. *Muhammad Speaks* reported the death of George Jackson as simply the deranged outcome of a prison-affected mentality. In the *The Black Panther,* however he was a hero while the same paper presented Sadat as a traitor of the Arab people. Of course, the Muslim paper declared Sadat a hero.

Obviously, both publications were slanted and perhaps only history will tell which was correct in relation to the well-being of the black community. At the time, we had to provide what we thought was the best possible presentation of news for our benefit, so we began to counteract the misinformation coming from *Muhammad Speaks*. We continued to put our newsletter out and address the issues from a different perspective, and sure enough, it wasn't long before our newsletter became a focal point for a lively debate. The main issue centered around the reporting of news from the black community and even coverage by the black media themselves. People started watching the news on the television and listening to the radio stations, most of which were white owned. News was being passed around the penitentiary with a higher interest. Soon, it was easy to find a group of prisoners standing around with both the Muslim and Panther papers open to some identical story and struggling over the issue.

We were always careful to maintain the close ties we had developed among the leadership of all the groups in the pen through struggle and support of their issues as well as ours. These debates were healthy and aided many prisoners in their quest to develop an understanding of the issues that affected our community. However, we made sure that there were no serious conflicts around issues in the newspapers, because we were all black men held in prison together under the same oppressive conditions. That was always the bottom line, and though our political differences were important, we never allowed them to become more important than our collective survival. The debates grew and so did the newsletter: it became a newspaper. We named it *The Panther Speaks*, and quickly got a number of prisoners involved in its production.

The paper contributed something significant to the population; for the first time, the men had a newspaper to which they could contribute their own writing. Those who had writing skills were soon submitting articles, while other prisoners acted as reporters, and still others gave up their time to type the paper up. Artists inside the prison walls drew cartoons and covers for the paper, while a crew of paperboys saw that everyone received a copy. A number of supportive individuals who saw the newspaper as their own gave whatever supplies and other materials they had to aid in the production of the paper. Its development was our response to administration's ban of progressive publications.

While we were producing our paper, another battle concerning first amendment rights of prisoners was underway on the legal front with the help of progressive lawyers and the legal aid project. We eventually won the right to receive all types of literature and reading materials in the Maryland prison system. Once we tested the court ruling by subscribing to a number of papers and finally receiving them, we discontinued the newspaper effort so that we could redirect our energy in other areas that needed attention.

This decision was a result of the need to step up organizing within the prison, but it proved unfortunate for those brothers who had developed skills in newspaper production, because they had to find other outlets for their talents. At the time, there was very little communication between us and other prisoners around the country, but we felt that things were happening inside of the prisons that we needed to know about. In some cases, we knew it was just important to keep lines of communication open with individuals in other prisons who were under the constant threat of physical attack, because to lose communication with them would have been emotionally and physically dangerous. We realized that the writers could best use their skills in that area while at the same time developing new and stronger contacts with other prison groups. And, indeed, the strong ties that developed between prisoners across the country would later prove very useful in national and international prison work.

Eddie (seated right) at the Maryland Penitentiary at an event co-sponsored by the Left Bank Jazz Society.

Members of the Maryland Penitentiary Inter-Communal Survival Collective.

Above: Eddie (second from right) participating in one of the many programs within the prison that he helped organize.
Previous page: Eddie with a participant in the To Say Their Own Words program.

Above: Eddie (at podium) and To Say Their Own Words at the Maryland Penitentiary.
Next page: Participants in the Friend of a Friend program in 2010. Dominque Stevenson at podium, Eddie immediately to her left.

Above: Eddie with his son, Deshawn, and his grandchildren.

Above: Eddie with his son, Ronald, and daughter-in-law, Monica.
Next page: Free Eddie Conway mural in Baltimore's Waverly neighborhood.

Chapter Nine

Of Riots and Resistance

July 17, 1972: Three young boys race their bicycles down the dark alley of the 500 block of East Eager Street. A set of eyes peek at them from the window that extends below ground level. The boys, in their haste, never once looked at the one-hundred-foot-high ugly gray brick building. Behind the peeking eyes stand three others, hard and desperate men seeking a universal objective. Freedom. Surrounding them in this ugly structure are some thirteen hundred prisoners going about their daily activities, unaware that their lives are about to change within the hour. The peering eyes are suddenly joined by another set as the boys speed off and race out of sight. "Let's get to moving," says a heavy voice in a very low tone. The two men work busily for the next five minutes trying to remove the three bars that stand between them and the dark street only feet away. The workers are having a bad time of it, while two other prisoners wait patiently for the bars to be removed. Time continues to pass, and other people begin to notice that something is out of order.

One thing after another goes wrong for the freedom seekers, because prisoners, like other oppressed people, are governed by Murphy's Law. The drill machine that the men are using blows up twice in the space of three minutes. This is before they are able to even put a dent in the bars. Next they try hacksaws that work only minimally at best. The process takes too long and the guards become aware that something is wrong in the windows. However, before they can raise the alarm the two men who had waited so patiently, so hopefully, and now in vain, step out from the shadows and take the officers captive with their homemade knives.

The die has been cast, and now other prisoners become involved in helping to capture additional guards who, though close by were still unaware of what was happening in the west wing. The stakes are suddenly higher, and a lot rides on getting the window bars cut before the guards in the other areas become aware of this bold attempt at liberation; to fail now is to perhaps fail forever. The outside situation is both favorable and at the same time unfavorable. A guard tower sits back behind a small white picket fence about five feet high and about fifty feet down the street from the window that the men are attempting to dismantle. The armaments in that tower could effectively control the whole area of Eager Street from any outside elements short of a tank.

At the same time, the lighting is poor and most of the bottom of the prison is dark, and the corners would effectively allow men to move within the shadows without much detection. If the prisoners could get out that window they would have a better than fair chance at making a successful escape into the night. The other men in the area recognized this and wanted to get in on the deal. Any number of prisoners could get away tonight and everyone is hopeful; some have already changed into street clothes and are hanging around watching the doors for any new guards who might foil their bid for freedom. The entire housing area has, by now, gotten word that the brothers are making a move and that there will soon be a hole in the window for anyone who wants to follow.

Things begin to quiet down in the west wing area, because the men know that they cannot hold the guards for too long without the phone security alerting the central control unit. The silence would permit the men to hear if an alarm was sounded, but the absence of noise in a block containing over two hundred and fifty cells and more than five hundred prisoners is peculiar, and the silence soon began to work against the men. The phones near the guard station began ringing, but there was no one there to answer them. The other guards undoubtedly wanted to know why the noise level had suddenly dropped. The half-dozen men who were now working each end of the bars still hoped that they could reach the streets before the guards could respond.

By this point, it had become apparent that something was awry, but the guards still didn't know exactly what was happening or how they should respond to it. The next few minutes were filled with anxiety for both sides. The guards knew that they had lost control of an area of the prison and had to respond immediately, but they had to do so carefully, so as not to cause a heightening of the tension, lest they risk the lives of the eight guards now held captive. The prisoners found themselves confronted with even higher stakes because they were either going to make it out, or they were going to face serious trouble because of their failure to do so.

Somewhere down on the flats, a small group of prisoners were already developing a back-up plan because they knew the resulting charges of kidnapping, attempted escape, and destruction of state property awaited them. Had any of the guards been hurt in the process of capture? It was unclear since they were being held in several different places, and no one seemed to know precisely what was happening where. Suddenly the alarm sounded, and the men knew that their time had come and gone; there was an entirely new situation brewing. Outside, the floodlights came on and the bottom areas of the building were bathed in light. Police patrol cars raced to the penitentiary and guards ran down Eager Street armed with rifles and shotguns as if they were in a face off with the ugly structure itself, weapons at the ready.

"Hey you in there," shouts a voice deepened by the bullhorn, as if uncertain what else to say, or to whom it is really speaking. "Hey you ... in there." A dozen spotlights shine into the building providing an awkward moment in the sun for the men who are imprisoned inside.

Leery of this new light, many of the prisoners who had waited in the shadows as the advance group attempted to loosen the bars that stood between them and freedom began to quickly disperse. The crowd changed quickly, as did the nature and intent of its actions. Other prisoners who were not a part of the escape attempt began to mill around the flats; they wanted part of this new action. Among them were men who had just a little time left to serve on their sentences, which made escape a lesser option, but, not liking the conditions they were living under, they were prepared to fight if a fight was coming. Other prisoners just wanted a piece of the action, something to shift their lives away from the monotony of living out year after year behind these bars. As the grouping changed, it became clear that the fight that would ensue would be more deadly than originally planned, especially as the men inside reacted toward the heavy firepower on the outside.

Some of the men inside had begun to release prisoners held in the RDCC unit, an area that housed more than five hundred men who were locked in cells all day long while they waited to be processed and shipped to other state institutions after classification. Many of these new men didn't know the rules governing prisoners, and this night had rushed into their lives out of the blue: one minute they were lying in their cells reading, writing, and talking through the doors to each other, when they suddenly found themselves in the middle of a riot. Some of these men, once they were released, began to take part in the revelry; they broke windows and smashed lights. Others began breaking into all the cabinets and lockers in their sight.

It wasn't long before a few old scores were settled and some new ones created. Any semblance of order was rapidly disappearing and no one was willing to take the reins of the riot, because it hadn't begun as a protest or a direct response to an act of the oppressors. All of the prisoners' organizations had withdrawn their members from the situation early on, and a small group of opportunists took charge. Some of them wanted to hang all the guards and kill all the informants while there was still a little time left; they, themselves, would fight to the death, they said. Another group among the rioters wanted to release all the guards; they were saving as many guards as they could find and hiding them from the others, a courageous act given the level of violence that was now surrounding them.

The cries that accompany beatings and attacks echoed up from the RDCC area as small bands of prisoners roamed about, attacking those prisoners who looked weak or isolated. As the force of the attacks increased, prisoners who tried to defend the isolated men became subject to attack themselves. Everyone was moving around with their face concealed, and with the captive guards now unable to protect some of the prisoners, rapes and robberies were taking place every few minutes. The lights were out—the result of the men's rampage—and the entire area was pitch-black. Only the areas that could be swept by the spotlight had any illumination, and when the spotlights focused on a single cell where an attack was occurring this would stop the attack in most cases, but the lights would have to move on and search out another attack, leaving the old victim to be attacked again.

While all of this was happening, there were ongoing negotiations to gain the release of the guards, even though the situation in the RDCC area had dissolved into violent abandon as gangs ten to fifteen strong roamed the tier brandishing pipes and homemade knives and feeding on the defenseless. Under the rotating glare of the spotlights, the end of the tier would reflect a little light only to be blacked out by many forms displaying all types of weapons. As these shadowy figures walked down the tier, they would look in each and every cell asking questions about everyone. Many of the men on RDCC knew someone who was in the prison, and in many cases these acquaintances had already gone over into the unit and pulled their friend or family member out of harm's way.

Those men who were left behind either had no ties to the other prisoners, or did not have anyone who cared enough about them to come to their aid. As the systematic questioning occurred, someone who knew somebody or could call the name of someone who might speak up for him might be left alone, and those who "carried" themselves like they were "okay" people might be able to avoid attack. The men who were singled out, unable to call the name of someone who might speak up for them, soon became the victim of the band who, in most cases, would assault or rape them. This was happening all over the RDCC, and in some areas of the general population as well. Time was running out for those inside the prison walls, yet the angry flames of rage burned on, threatening to erupt into an inferno right in the heart of the city. The anger that fueled the prisoners was a timeless sort of fury, born of too many lifetimes of injustice and dehumanization. Unfortunately, the walls had closed in on the prisoners and, as happens sometimes with the oppressed, they victimized the powerless among them.

It seemed like an eternity, for there had been no real beginning to the riot and neither did the end appear to be close at hand for those who were suffering; yet it had only been two hours since the boys first rode past on their bicycles. Timelessness did not exist for the prison administration, they were painfully aware of every minute that they did not have control of the entire prison. An attack was being prepared and revenge hung heavy in the air. From the other side of the doors leading into the west wing area came the sound of barking dogs and guard units preparing for the attack; also highly visible were the police lines moving into the prison complex. The noise level grew as the police, guards, and state troopers gathered together and milled around outside the doors.

Everyone knew they were merely waiting for the order to pounce, so the prisoners had erected massive barriers down on the flats made of any materials that they could lay their hands on. Perhaps as many as one hundred men manned the barricades armed with makeshift weapons of every sort. What had just minutes earlier been a chaotic situation was now shaping into a concerted effort to defend the population, when suddenly the flats were rocked by a loud explosion. This noise did not deter the several prisoners who were stationed on top of the various housing areas which were about twenty-five or thirty feet apart. These men were armed with projectiles that were to be thrown down upon the invaders. Between the door and the barricades there existed a virtual "no man's land" where a fight would soon take place. A series of explosions sounded as the doors flew open and about fifteen dogs charged the barriers. The animals were followed closely by guards hurling gas grenades and smoke grenades at the barricades; they went off in every direction. The dogs had leapt the barricades and were attacking individual prisoners.

The two lines, prisoner and police, came together in a pitched battle; it was short-lived. The stun guns in the hands of the police were the deciding factor in the situation. These weapons found their mark in most cases, and the victim would be forcefully carried away from the area, temporarily disabled and unable to offer any resistance. The guards moved up the tiers to lock down the prison, quickly clearing the area of prisoners. They would gain control of each level as they traveled upward. This process moved from tier to tier with the guards stopping at each cell. They would ask who lived there and determine whether the prisoner wanted to be locked in. Those remaining people who were on the tier, but not housed there, would be pushed off the other end and forced to run with the rest of the fleeing individuals. The newly freed guards were now pointing out the people who had held them captive. Several of them were selecting not only the prisoners they knew to be involved, but including any other men who had given them trouble in the past, or worse, those that they *thought* might have been involved.

The impact that this situation had on the prison was significant; a whole new set of security devices would result. Guard posts were placed in each wing, such that no one could physically reach the guards ever again. About thirty-seven prisoners were charged for inciting the riot, the kidnap of guards, and the resulting attacks upon prisoners from the

RDCC unit. A number of other prisoners were moved to minimum security institutions as a reward for providing information to the administration before, during, or after the riot. As suddenly as it had occurred, it was over; a riot staged in the shadow of a failed attempt at freedom by a few prisoners. The lack of leadership had lead to massive internal violence among the prisoners.

This was much the same thing that we were seeing in black communities outside the prison walls, where many of the leaders had been removed—murdered or locked up, for the most part—by the government, and replaced with imposters who had no real intent of addressing the issues that the people were facing. In the absence of the guidance and direction of leaders who represented the best interest of the community, our youth, some of whom had internalized that same rage that all oppressed people carry around, began to turn on each other, having never been provided with any other appropriate outlet. This self-destruction is endemic among the oppressed; it demonstrates how violence, the primary tool of the oppressor, has been internalized by the victims. Had we paid attention then, we would have known that it was all a reflection of things to come. Indeed, almost all of the prisoners attacked on the RDCC that night were either white or gay; the majority of their attackers turned out to be black.

Chapter Ten

The Collective

Of the original membership of the Panther organization that was in place when I arrived at the penitentiary, only twenty-five survived the process of political education and training. We became the Maryland Penitentiary Inter-Communal Survival Collective (MPISC). All of my organizing in the early years was in league with MPISC members. Although networking and building alliances both inside and outside the prison walls was always a priority, those of us in the Collective who were organizing within the prison always made a point of training of our members in the martial arts whenever possible, primarily in secret. We had to constantly relocate our training areas for a number of reasons, mainly due to issues of security and secrecy. We would shift the training from area to area to keep non-Collective personnel from observing our tactics and training program. On the other hand, we had to do this to keep from going on lockup since it was illegal to train in self-defense. It was this moving around in out-of-the-way places that caused us to be in the basement of the "G" building one morning. We had been using the area for more than three weeks, at least two to three times a week. In reality we should have changed areas at the end of the second week, but the location was ideal because someone would have to get the elevator and go down to the basement to observe the training, which greatly reduced the possibility of our being discovered.

Everyone knew that the area was caged up and off limits, so no one went there. Once we got into the basement, we could send the elevator back upstairs and really get a good workout, but we had to remain there until one of the comrades brought the elevator back down. Normally there was no need to worry about anyone, whether guards or prisoners, getting into this area, or at least that's what we thought. On this particular morning, we were working out when there was a power failure. Well, we knew that meant a problem for us, but we had no idea the amount of trouble it would cause.

An electrician came down into the area by a hidden door on the other side of the building. Since we couldn't see what was actually over on that side, we could never have known that a tunnel existed there. For his part, he thought we were trying to escape, which got us all placed on lockup. The charges were eventually reduced to being out of bounds, since we were not in the tunnel area, and we really hadn't known about it. The prison officials didn't want anyone in the population to believe that there were, in fact, tunnels under the Maryland Penitentiary, so they couldn't charge us with something they denied existed. We did receive four months on lockup for being out of bounds and that made our future choice of exercise areas much more selective. But it wasn't long after we got off lockup that an even more serious situation developed. Our membership soon came under attack.

The only thing Bobby Mack recalled when he woke up in the hospital was seeing the ground rush up towards him, and the sound of the pipe smashing into his head. He was locked up and placed in the administration segregation unit. After thirty days, he was released back into the general population. No one knew what had happened to him or why. Early the next morning as the prisoners poured out of the west wing on the way to their job assignments, everything seemed peaceful and quiet for the new day. I walked up the path alone and fairly relaxed. Bobby stood leaning against the railed fence. He called me and since I knew him, I never gave the situation another thought. I did notice that he was carrying a cup in one hand and wearing a heavy jacket during rather warm weather.

Beyond that, I really paid no attention to him at that point. It was only after he started talking that I realized right away that something was seriously wrong. Once you spent time in the prison setting, you start to be able to pick up on the moods of people in seconds. This brother appeared highly agitated, and scared on top of that. He was saying things like "I haven't done anything to you, why are you planning this," and, "I thought we were alright." I became immediately alert and shifted to a defensive position while checking him over visually for weapons or any other materials that might be harmful to me. I was really caught off guard because here was a person that really felt threatened by me and I was not aware of any reason that he should be. The brother seemed shaken, so I tried to put him at ease as I began to question him, asking him what he felt was going on and how he came to hold those ideas.

He soon told me that someone had informed him that I had placed a hit on him, and that he was to die that very day in the music room. Consequently, I learned from him that it was rumored that the first attack was supposed to have been ordered by me also. The brother had been on some type of medication down in the psychological clinic. They had fed him this story while he was medicated in the hopes of him acting on their information without giving it a second thought. I was really getting hot about the situation because I still saw it for what it was: an official effort to have me killed in the yard by another prisoner without the least threat or provocation. Bobby had a long history of violence on his record and this would just be another case. He was undergoing treatment in the psychological clinic and was not only isolated from the general population, but he was also from out of state. He was the perfect scapegoat for a murder rap. Thankfully, though, the officials had made two mistakes in their selection of him. I had actually met this brother when I was in city jail, and had spent some time helping him out because he was out of state; he was from New Jersey. I bought him a carton of cigarettes because some other prisoners had stolen his. I found out who had done this and got his smokes back, and he had always respected me as a Panther and a person because I had stood up for him. He was always a little strange, even then, and probably needed treatment for some form of mental illness. He had become increasingly violent over the years, and that made him a good choice to carry out the hit, but our previous history had motivated him to talk this through with me.

Second, he liked the Black Panther Party and that gave me an edge. If I had been someone else, he informed me later, I would have been attacked without a warning or second thought. Recently, one of the comrades had been attacked just like that by another out-patient from the psychological clinic. At the time, we thought it was an isolated incident, but now a second patient was telling me that Lieutenant "D" took him around the corner about thirty minutes prior and warned him to be careful and watch out for me because his life was in danger. Once he understood that he was being used by the administration to attack me, he wanted to attack the lieutenant, who was, at the time, somewhere off at the other end of the prison waiting to hear them call a code red. I told him that first we should confront this Lieutenant "D" together and see what he had to say about this before we decided on any course of action.

So we went, and we confronted this pig together, and he was obviously shocked and terrified. The look on his face told us that we had caught this fish out of water. After we demanded an explanation, he told us that he had received a number of informant's notes the previous night, which said that something like this was going to happen. I had several questions: What was he was doing in the prison last night since he was a day shift officer, and why he had not offered the brother some protection, or if he really thought the brother was in trouble, why didn't he lock me up? Finally, I asked him why he had not confronted both of us about the situation.

Threats and counter-threats are made between prisoners all the time and the correct way of dealing with them is to call both parties in and have them sign body waivers after a peace agreement has been reached. None of this happened in this case, because there just simply weren't any threats in the first place. I read Lieutenant "D" the riot act, and let him know that if any more attacks or attempts were made on myself or any other member of the Collective in the near future, he would personally be held responsible and treated accordingly, inside or outside or whatever the situation called for. The leadership of the Collective decided to make the warden and other officials aware of the situation involving Lieutenant "D," who was part of the racist clique that was working night and day to create violence among the black prisoners. Afterward, things quieted down for a couple of months.

July can be notoriously hot in Baltimore, but on this day, July 12, 1973, the weather was mild; in no way did it hint at the hell that was about to break loose. Six or seven comrades gathered in the cell that we had designated the unofficial headquarters of the Maryland Penitentiary Inter-Communal Survival Collective. The back half of the fifth tier also housed our library and office, all, of course, unofficial. Housed on this level were also several of our members. It was the highest tier in the prison and the farthest away from all surveillance. We operated our survival programs, physical education classes, and martial arts training from this area.

Down below on the flats, an event was beginning to play out that would have an effect on the entire prison system in Maryland. It wasn't any different from the hundreds or perhaps thousands of nearly identical events that had already occurred within that tomb. The beating of a black man was a regular thing in the history of that place; it was as if it was a required sacrifice to sustain the structure. However, this day would be different. There was a new revolutionary organization in the prison and self-defense was a part of the platform for the group. Our organization based its principles on those of the Black Panther Party, and the member's primary concern was for the welfare of the community within the prison.

I had been in the prison for over a year and a half at this point, and I had spent much of that time on lockup, so I had never seen the guards administer one of their notorious beat downs in front of dozens of witnesses as they were on this day. Most of the beatings that I was aware of had taken place in the "hole," the isolated block of five or six cells where punishment was meted out on a regular basis to the rebellious men within the prison's ranks. The only other prisoners allowed into that area were those responsible for serving food and performing janitorial duties. The word would swirl among the population that this prisoner or that prisoner received a beating, but most felt powerless to do anything about the situation. It became acceptable and many saw it as just another part of the brutal prison culture. Guards beat prisoners with a guaranteed impunity and this practice never even raised an eyebrow.

The culture of violence that existed within this structure had direct ties to slavery and oppression, as did the culture of resistance that would soon result in a direct response to this particular abuse. The guards formed an entourage of sorts, their attendant business being to kick and beat the man that they were dragging past hundreds of prisoners. The prisoners who were on the flats or in their cells on the first and second tiers were outraged. The men began to throw objects at the guards and those who lacked physical objects threw slurs. Each side made threats back and forth as the guards continued to brutalize their captive. When, finally, they threw him into lockup, satisfied that he no longer posed a threat, they went back and singled out one of the other prisoners who had protested too loudly.

Suddenly, there were other guards acting as reinforcements and responding to what they took to be a riot in the making. Those prisoners targeted for retribution from the goon squad, which had started the situation in the first place, were isolated behind a locked grill. The guards allowed the other prisoners to leave the area. It was at this point that a comrade found his way up to our "office" and informed us of the developments below. One of those locked behind the grill, Rob Folks was a leader in the Maryland Penitentiary Inter-Communal Survival Collective. Rob was much like George Jackson: an intense brother who worked well with the population and he was well received by most. Rob had been the most vocal among those protesting the beating and now he refused to back down when the reinforcements attempted to neutralize the situation.

A group of us had arrived on the scene at almost the same time as the original group of guards who had come back to settle with Folks and the others who had opposed the beating. One group of guards blocked the grill while another group approached Folks, attempting to attack him from behind. Several comrades began to engage the guards who were blocking the grill, forcing it open while the other comrades gained entrance into the area where Folks was trapped. We collided with the guards who were behind Folks, and in the violence that ensued, the guard who had been in charge of the beating that had precipitated this incident received several stab wounds. This battle continued for a few minutes longer, until finally the guards retreated, allowing the comrades to leave the area. Later, they returned to retrieve their fallen member.

For a brief time, everything came to a standstill. The comrades had blended back into the population, and most of the prisoners were in that mental place where one goes after winning the battle. When this moment passed, it became clear that this minor victory would not appease the war gods. During that brief moment, the guards experienced the shock that occurs when the eye of the bully has been blackened, and he is sent running. They were not accustomed to organized resistance. This was not a riot with the chaos and calamity that those situations usually bring, neither was it a gang fight or a situation in which the guards could isolate one side or exploit the divisions. Above all, it was not what they had expected when they had made their way through the prison with a beaten man in tow. Predictably, their response would be severe, and all these years later, I am still haunted by the depravity that they exhibited.

After the administration had sent for and received sufficient reinforcements, the prison was shut down and everyone was locked in their cells.

Payback was in the air and on the tongues of the guards and we knew that the Collective would take a hit. Five comrades, including Folks and I, were singled out for the retributive punishment that gets served up in hefty portions in prison whenever the existing status quo is challenged and, in this case, flipped on its head, if only for a moment. They rounded us up and one by one took us to the hole where we were beaten.

The area was crowded with the bodies of men who no longer looked like men; they had taken on the characteristics of pigs by this point. Greedy with revenge, it was evident that they would maul anyone who fell into the pen. I was thrown in. The attacks started immediately and continued until I was no longer conscious, and probably beyond. When finally I awoke, I was in great pain. My jaw and shoulder had been broken, and my head was busted. I felt as if my brain would seep out of my head as I alternated between consciousness and sleep. The bruises and lacerations that covered my entire body simply served as background pain. I have no idea of what I must have looked like at that point, but judging from the pain, it must have been monstrous.

Days passed by and I lay in pain, completely isolated and unable to identify the place that they were holding me. I did know that I had never seen this part of the prison, and later I would learn that it was the old death row section of the penitentiary, which housed the gas chamber and the cells of the condemned. They held me there in that remote section of the prison without the benefit of medical treatment for a number of days clearly hoping I would die from the injuries. I could not communicate with the outside world, and the administration did not allow anyone into the prison to see me. Finally, my lawyer got a court order to see me, and once she saw the state I was in, she insisted that they rush me to the hospital for emergency treatment. I was there for a month, and upon release I joined my comrades on lockup. Though the other four had also suffered through the guards' brutality, I was the only one they had tried to kill. This was the first of several attempts that they would make on my life.

Eventually the administration transferred the five of us to Patuxent, a prison that provides mental health evaluations and treatment. I guess they thought we must have been crazy, because resistance is often perceived as insane, even by people of color. The experience at Patuxent showed me first-hand how the pharmaceutical companies were using prisoners to test their new medications. I also noted that, in this prison, the population of whites was more in proportion to their actual number in the state population, while the penitentiary was already beginning to show signs of a black majority. From the very inception of the Maryland Penitentiary in 1811, the incarceration rate of blacks was twice that of whites.

After about three months at Patuxent, the Department of Corrections returned us to solitary lockup at the Maryland Penitentiary. We would spend two and a half years on lockup; this was the first time that anyone in the prison system received more than a year's sentence at one time on lockup. Other prisoners had received more than a year's time on lockup, but only after receiving a new sentence while serving a sentence. Clearly, the "powers that be" were sending a message to other prisoners: revolt and we will bury you. They had failed to kill us, so they would shove us into the recesses of the prison.

In retrospect, it seemed as if they were trying to shove us back into the womb, into some form of nonexistence. This is what prisons do to people of color, especially men. The design of the institution is to create a permanent state of infancy in which the individual is vulnerable and dependent. However, for those of us who had seen manhood in the absolute sense—self-determination and self-defense—there was no going back. Members of the Collective continued to organize other prisoners while on lockup. We focused largely on political education, and on helping many brothers to develop interpersonal communication skills. Soon, the entire lockup area was our own university and training center.

Still, it is a painful existence to live as an animal, caged in a six-by-nine-foot cell for two and a half years. Life moves fast outside the prison walls, and it is hard for the prisoner on lockup to maintain even a few close relationships. It becomes more difficult for the visitor to reach the prisoner, and the physical constraints serve as painful reminders of the prisoner's powerlessness. The pain of delivering a kiss through the phone, hands separated from touch by glass, the pain reflected through each other's eyes, all of these things remain long after the visit is over. Finally, there are fewer visits and eventually family relationships and friendships succumb to even more layers of steel and concrete. I missed so many things during this time, it was as if the community disappeared, and after a while, I even struggled to remember what family members looked like. Finding it impossible to keep up with the people I knew, I turned to the struggles that were going on in the world, and began to educate myself.

During this three-year period, I read more books than at any other period in my life. Many of these books covered black history, philosophy, military science, and world history. Prison inadvertently provides the imprisoned with an opportunity for rebirth. I had spent most of my time up to this point dealing with conditions and being on the defensive, so this period afforded me the opportunity to reflect and broaden my world perspective, and it influenced how I would work for years to come. I learned enough to ensure that I would no longer approach the problems of oppression and white supremacy simply from a defensive stance. From this ordeal, I would become a more spiritual being, connected to the world, its people and struggles, but sadly, less connected to my family. It is impossible to compensate for what I missed with my family. Nevertheless, upon my release from lockup, I was more prepared and determined to begin a new round of struggle. This time I would train and educate my fellow prisoners to free themselves and our community.

For the most part, the beatings stopped in the penitentiary after this incident, or at least, the acceptability of the brutality did. Personally, the cost was high, but the price had to be paid. There are still instances of beatings behind closed doors or in the heat of a battle, and of course, those of a retaliatory nature, but by and large, beatings would become something of the past. In place of the physical "controls," they would employ new "tools" to manage the population, and in some cases, they were the same ones that help to manage and control the population outside of prisons. Television, extended family visits and special events, and exposure to technology such as computers and word processors, and now even video games help to control prisoners. All of these spread throughout the system here in Maryland.

Chapter Eleven

The Bowels of Hell

It was sometime in 1977 when Kay said to me, in that way that women do when they are calling you on your responsibility, "You need to talk to your son." I knew that she was right; he was fast becoming a young adult and prison had put too much space between us. Kay and I had separated before I was imprisoned, and because of the fact that I was often on lockup during the first seven years of my incarceration, I had not seen her or Ronald very much. During those years, I was in survival mode, and consequently had given very little thought to parenting, though my son had always been in my heart. Yet, I knew it was time to become a father and the relationship between child and parent was such that the boundaries of prison walls did not exist, though they were always there.

Fatherhood had been for me an odd state of being in which, on one hand I had always been proud of the human beings I had helped to create, but, on the other hand, I was nagged by concerns about the lives my children would lead and how the world would treat them. In addition, imprisonment offers more than its share of complications for the parent who is behind bars. Ronald was doing what many teens at that time were doing—drinking, hanging out in the streets, and running with his "boys." I'm sure he was giving Kay the blues, though she never admitted it.

I recalled my own teen years; I was not rebellious with my parents, but I'm certain that some of my exploits caused them to worry. Looking back now, I clearly see how, as a young man, I had failed to look at how my actions would impact others. I had been in search of myself, and I had taken a few wrong turns along the way. When I found out that my son was in the midst of the throes of that same search for self, I felt happy and proud for a moment. After that, I grew concerned. Would Ronald make the same mistakes and experience the same mishaps that I had? The world was not the place it had been when I was growing up. It only took one look at the growing prison population to confirm that.

I wanted Ronald to continue to grow and to have those experiences in life that make us wise, but not before his time, and I wanted to guide him along the way. So I made a decision that would bring us closer together. One of the community programs that the comrades and I had developed was a ten-week counseling program for youth who were troubled and at high risk of coming into the criminal justice system. Some of the young people were court-appointed, but parents inside and outside of the prison could request help from this program. Well, this turned out to be one of the few times that I actually *needed* a program that I had implemented.

I asked Cheryl Waters, a close friend and schoolteacher to bring Ronald to the program. She would pick him up from home once a week and bring him to the prison for the sessions, and then return him to his home in the evening. This gave me the opportunity to talk to my son for two hours each week without the guards hovering or the other barriers to our communication that were presented by the visiting room.

I had always tried to let Ronald make his own decisions and now it became even more important for him to make his own choices in life, but I was determined to be able to influence him enough to make healthy ones. My own experience had taught me that when we are young we might listen to the advice of elders, but when it came down to it, we would still do what we thought was best for ourselves. I wanted to be supportive of whatever Ronald wanted to do with his life. My approach was to discuss whatever Ronald wanted to talk about, and then look at any possible choices he could make. We would examine things from both the positive and negative perspective and then discuss his thoughts.

Sometimes we would just sit there quietly for a time, while Ronald decided on a course of action. Those were some of the best times for me because they gave me a sense of humanness in the midst of what is really an abnormal and inhumane environment. The joy of watching my son grow, and not just in physical terms but emotionally and intellectually, coupled with the fact that I was guiding him into adulthood, was priceless.

Though Ronald has gone on to achieve many things, I have never been as proud of him as I was in that moment when I watched him ponder his future and become a man. All these years later, looking over his shoulder as he teaches at Bowling Green State University in Ohio, I like to think that in some small way I helped give him that chance. I have helped numerous other young people along the way, but obviously none of those situations has been as rewarding as this experience with Ronald.

Meanwhile, tension was building again in the prison and sleepless nights had become routine for some members of the population. A heavy slumber would remain elusive as long as this electricity crackled throughout the prison, sparking fights in its wake.

"Fire!"

Someone yelled the words out deep in the night, and it was as if all of those emotional sparks had finally caught on and threatened to consume the prison. I must confess, I have learned to sleep through what most people might find unimaginable—stabbings, fights, and all types of noise—and this night was no exception. I was awakened by my cell buddy, who informed me that the fire was burning several doors up from us. The guards were unable to open the door to the burning cell because they were not allowed to have keys upstairs after midnight. This regulation was a result of the 1972 riot.

All the keys for the cellblocks were locked in the guard's post desk, to be given out by a lieutenant. So the fire burned out of control. They had to run downstairs to the guard post to get the keys, and by the time they got back flames were leaping from the cell making it impossible to approach the door. The fire-fighting equipment was so old and useless that it had little effect on the fire. The cells in the Maryland Penitentiary had been painted hundreds of times in as many years, causing a build-up on the walls that was so heavy that you could dig for hours and never see the steel wall. In most cases, no one ever tried to clean the old paint away once they moved into a cell. The occupant would simply get some paint and redo the cell the way they wanted it to look. This paint was highly flammable, and once ablaze it was almost impossible to put out.

Thus, the cell had become completely engulfed in flames and the lack of fire hoses on the housing units made this a situation of criminal proportions. Amongst the thirteen hundred men housed in the facility, there were only a small number of hand-held fire extinguishers and no heavy fire-fighting equipment at all. The locks themselves dated back to the 1930s and had to be opened one at a time. This greatly impacted the situation because it meant that the guards had to come in close contact with the fire in order to release the now very desperate men who were caged in those cells. Over half the prisoners on the tier were still trapped in their cells and the panic was spreading. Worse yet, the guards were also running around in a state of confusion, not certain what action they should take. The minutes lost could easily mean lives lost. There didn't seem to be enough keys to immediately release everyone, and all the prisoners in the cells above and below were now frantic.

Eventually, the guards managed to get the fire under control, but two members of the New Family gang were killed in the fire, a godfather and a lieutenant. There was immediate suspicion that this was a "hit," and the population was on edge. The prison administration would experience the real inferno the following day because we were all mad as hell by the time we got out of those cells. Several protests were staged the next day, and the list of issues was long: the lack of access to the keys to unlock the doors at night, the absence of fire-fighting equipment in the prison and the fact that it really had not been noticed before, as well as the paint build-up. The fact that the guards had to go all the way back down to the guard station to get the keys to open the cell rather than having a lever throwing device at the end of the tier to free people in the event of an emergency was yet another issue that need to be addressed. An automatic opening device would have saved lives and freed other prisoners from their cells instead of trapping them inside where they suffered from smoke inhalation.

That so many men had found themselves trapped in their cells nagged at us all. We all wondered what would happen if more than one cell was on fire at the same time, since we had barely escaped from this fire. Suddenly, the tension between the various groups of prisoners had been replaced with serious concern and discussion about fire safety. These discussions spread across the yard like a current and, finally, there was a flat refusal to return to those cells until someone could guarantee that the locking devices would be changed. The word on the yard was that a number of complaints had been made to the officials in recent months, but most had gone unanswered. By the time the warden got into the yard, the men were worked up and they began to hurl question after question at him. This resulted in a shouting session, and nothing was resolved, however the warden agreed to meet with a group of representatives from the population.

Unfortunately, the meeting only proved that there was a gross lack of communication between us and the prison administration. It was agreed that we needed an ongoing forum to deal with the issues that kept popping up and remained largely unresolved. The way to deal regularly was through something like an inmate advisory committee. The warden agreed to allow such a committee to be set up, and promised a regular monthly meeting with such a body of prisoners to deal with agreed upon agendas. The other issues were to be worked on and, by the time we met again, the administration would answer questions about the locking devices and the other issues, and we would have a charter and some by-laws to govern the formulation of any advisory committee.

So, we went back to the population with the information, and things were somewhat under control at this point. We got started on the paperwork for the Inmate Advisory Committee, because we knew that one of the conditions was that all of the paperwork had to be approved by the warden before we would be allowed to officially operate as a body of prison representatives, and this could become a delaying tactic. There would be an election and one-year terms, and all of this would require a six-month waiting period. We got together and, after some discussion, it was agreed that it would be even better if the population had an organized structure to deal with the administration in future encounters. One thing we wanted was to have more control over the funds and the programs that were coming into the penitentiary. We also wanted to communicate directly with the administration without having to go through the "on the yard" act of resistance every few months. The situation always held the potential for violence and never resolved anything anyway until we met with the officials, so why not just establish a means of dealing with them on a regular basis?

Once we got the charter and by-laws approved, we set up the election for the coming month. I did not run for any of the official positions because of all the double-talk and bullshit that was required to deal with the administration. But because I had been one of the regular prison leaders who had originally been selected to meet with the warden after the fire, I had to continue acting as a part of the ad hoc advisory committee until the six-month time period was over and the elected officers could take their positions. As a result of the original situation on the yard that day after the fire, the tension was still very high and a lot of little beefs were developing between the prisoners and the guards. The officials tried to distract the population from the real issues, so they used the fire to manipulate the situation for their own interests. Soon, it was being suggested that the fire was started as part of a gang war. The officials went a step further and locked up a number of people from different groups, gangs, and organizations. They finally put the word out that the Collective was behind this hit, and soon they locked up one of our members and he was held incommunicado.

The rumors that went around the yard ranged from the story that the fire was the result of a hit that I had ordered, to the smoking in bed theory. The bigger problem was that there was a lot of tension, as well as a struggle for leadership, in the New Family gang which resulted in a lot of talk about hitting someone back. At the time, I don't even think they cared who they struck out at, so long as they took some action. The leadership of the Collective was in the spotlight and we had to be very careful how we handled this situation. We had to take some time out and meet with a number of groups and factions of the gang to set the record straight. While this was going on, the officials continued to fan the flames in hopes that an incident would take some of the heat off of them. The newspapers were asking the same questions that we had asked about the locking system and the lack of a prevention program; heads were going to roll and things were looking bad for the administration.

The situation in the yard was rather tight for a few days after the incident, since the gang leader who died had been, in fact, one of the administration's key informants. Their other informants were scared to death that they would be next, so they were more than willing to help the administration move on the Collective's membership. The information being put out by these informants and "unofficially" by the "officials" was beginning to take root and create problems. Much debate was going on in the yard about the right or wrong of such attacks. There were a few hotheads on both sides, and many were feeding into the rumors out of fear, anger, or ignorance. Yet, the general population knew the real story and refused to be played by the officials and their use of informants. The potential for violence was very high, but there was not a single incident in the yard among the prisoners.

The New Family had been, and remained, one of the administration's main tools in the prison, but the fact of the matter was that it had also gotten completely out of hand. It was increasingly difficult for the administration to keep them in check. New members were trying to gain leadership and move the gang into the drug game. Up until that point, the gang had been involved in small-time stuff, like wine-making. Now the drug game was a problem for the administration, since the profits could be used to corrupt the guard force, which was always ready to do anything for a few dollars. Since the Family had aided the administration in its effort to stop the union drive, and had helped keep the youthful population involved in gang wars rather than politics, the officials turned a blind eye to their activities.

Once the drugs started to come in, there was pressure put on the faction that was into the drug scene. The different gangs in the prison made something like fire bombing very likely. And although the different gangs and the Collective had been in conflicts before, very few physical contacts were made simply because the Collective was always working in the interests of the general population and a little gang of killers didn't stand a chance in the face of the popular support we had. We were just too strong for anyone to want any trouble from us, and in turn, we never tried to deal with the gangs or cliques on any level other than to educate them.

Our members were the bad dudes in the prison long before they became members, so we didn't have anything to prove. The members all had spent months and years in training in the martial arts and teaching others these skills. The ties and connections we had developed throughout the prison were very strong. Many of the other organizations in the prison were able to organize and develop because of our support during their initial formation, so we had very strong ties to almost all the organizations that had structure and discipline. And, finally, the Collective was *always* working in the interest of the population. That won us no less than a hundred active supporters so our numbers were very great in the general population of thirteen hundred. For all those reasons, Collective members rarely found themselves in physical combat with anybody, gangs or individuals. The respect for the Collective was very high and only from time to time did minor conflicts between individual members develop. These beefs would usually be worked out by a group of friends and associates of the principals involved. Very rarely was there an actual fight or the use of physical force. Now, it was a known fact that the Collective continued to work against what we thought were the disruptive and negative influences of the New Family. The forced participation of newly arrived youth into the drug and sex culture of the gang was actively opposed through our education programs and individual rap sessions with the new arrivals. On the other hand, because we continued to be the group in the forefront of most of the organizing in the prison, we stepped on a lot of toes, most often offending those involved in drug dealing, because this was counter to what we wanted for our community and the future of our youth. We knew that there was a need for better communication among members the prison population.

Thus, the first major seminar we put together in the penitentiary was organized around the need for communication development. The staff of the prison library played a key role in the effort to organize this seminar and bring together members of the Baltimore community and the prison population. The planning and coordinating was done by a small group of politically conscious prisoners working closely with a very progressive librarian, and with outside community supporters who also came from a progressive background. The seminar brought together a number of communications and media specialists from the surrounding community and a number of prisoners with a strong interest in communicating among ourselves and with the world outside. Many of the individuals involved with our newspaper were also involved with the seminar.

The event took place in the auditorium and over a hundred and fifty people attended. The four-day-long program was broken up into a series of workshops that focused on four key areas: a newspaper for the prison, a television station for the prison, a radio station for the prison, and the development of more programs to benefit the population. On the fifth day, we reconvened as a group and devoted most of the time to reports from the various workshops, and followup discussions. We were asking for a commitment from the prisoners and outside guests to continue the work that was begun during the seminar, and to support future initiatives. One of the most important things that came out of that seminar was a lasting network of media and communications experts who continued to support us in our efforts to develop progressive media and outreach programs.

Though the goals of the seminar were large ones, they weren't entirely out of the realm of possibility; in 1978 television and radio stations were a reality in other prisons, and we wanted to develop our media program along similar lines. The possibility existed for us to create in-house programming, and to do closed-circuit broadcasting of both television and radio, strictly within the prison walls. And the sad fact of the matter is that the officials agreed to allow us the opportunity to set up these programs within the next six months, and then reneged on their commitment to us. Not to be deterred, we continued to work towards getting a class set up and having instructors brought in who would teach journalism courses to a small group of us who would then publish an official penitentiary newspaper. We successfully completed the courses and established a newspaper in the prison—not the first one, of course, but the first *official* one.

We also established our own courses on radio programming and set up our own radio station *un*officially. Each night, we would come on the air at 11:30, and broadcast until midnight. Every couple of days, it would be moved to another location. As it turned out, the whole seminar process was a good one for planning, organizing, and carrying out programs and activities in the prison. We continued to carry on other work in different areas, with different ends in mind. Of course, the conditions of the penitentiary never got any better, no matter how hard we worked on them. It seemed like they were built into the system. The level of oppression, the conditions unfit for human habitation—these were institutionalized already. There were times when it honestly seemed like nothing would or could work to change the conditions we were living with.

The more we organized, the more the officials tried to disrupt our efforts. Among members of the general prison population, it seemed that no one cared about these conditions or the level of oppression that prisoners experienced on a daily basis. It was out of fashion and no longer the thing to do in law-and-order-America. The left was losing the ability to organize support for radical issues and the community at large was starting to feel the impact of the massive FBI misinformation programs about prisoners and radical groups. Being very supportive of prisoners' groups was a risky business at that time in America. The public newspapers were working overtime to print negative stories about prisoners and the criminal element in general. The positive things we were doing were receiving no exposure at all. The things that the guards were doing to us were largely unreported or reported in a light that made the guards' behavior seem reasonable, or as though they were the only course of action under the conditions.

We had to find a way to get our side of the story out to the public in general or at the very least, to some individuals on the outside we felt might be able to exert a degree of control over our situation. We decided to send out periodic newsletters to elected officials and community leaders to keep them informed of the happenings inside the prison. These would be professional newsletters with detailed information, dealing with anything that affected us specifically, or with the general conditions within the prison. Our objective was two-fold: first, this was a way of keeping representatives and community leaders informed about our situation. Second, the publicity would put the administration under the spotlight and, we hoped, cause them to check some of their actions and behavior toward the prisoners.

This effort, although secret, involved a great many people on the level of information-gathering. We had to steal records, orders, and memos from the offices and desks of the prison officials, get them copied, and put them back when we could. Their most loyal trustees did most of that stealing, and the results were explosive. We exposed the misuse of funds designated for the welfare of indigent prisoners—there were tens of thousands of dollars paid to guards that should have been going toward the welfare of prisoners. This had been going on for years and the soap or toothpaste that we should have received never got there because the funds were going elsewhere. We also exposed a white supremacist clique within the prison guards, which had been working together with a group of racist prisoners to distribute hate materials and real weapons among the prison population, with the intent of creating confrontations between the white racist organization and the black prisoners. We managed to uncover information on the clique amongst the guards, as well as information about its leaders and their relationship to the KKK, and we made these facts known in one of our newsletters.

We also began to notice that there was something strange going on with a number of prisoners who were undergoing psychiatric treatment in the prison hospital. At least twice a week, one of the prisoners would attack another prisoner for no apparent reason. The attacks were random and did not seem to have any basis. We would be sitting in the mess hall eating and a prisoner would get up and walk over to another prisoner with his tray, take the tray and hit the other man in the head repeatedly. Once this was stopped, the prisoner under attack would be shocked, because he simply couldn't think of anything that could have provoked the attack. Almost a dozen of these incidents occurred before we could put enough pressure on the psychological ward to stop using these prisoners to maintain a level of violence, so that they could justify their continuing demands for more funds. Guards and key officials were also using some of these mentally unstable individuals to attack selective targets among the population. There were a number of attacks directed toward the members of progressive organizations, in particular members of the Collective. The newsletter was instrumental in helping us to get the word out about this situation.

The impact of those newsletters can never really be determined, but it is safe to say that, shortly after the one on the psychological treatment ward, these attacks stopped altogether, or rather dropped back down to a normal level. We noticed real changes, and saw real reactions to the newsletters. The information on the misuse of welfare funds was later used to file a court case about the issue. The administration made a lot of efforts to clean up the area we were writing about.

We also discovered that illiteracy was a real problem within the prison population and started working to address it. In my opinion, it's the job of everyone who expresses concern for their people to teach as many of their community members as possible to read and write, to think and make decisions for themselves. To me, it seems that repressive political systems control the flow and development of most organizations by controlling who can do what, where, and how in these organizations. Therefore, the task of the activist is to aid in the development of a cadre among the oppressed people, who will work in their interest and for their goals.

Over the years, many political activists have asked themselves the question of where to find the people who will be trained to do this type of work. Answers have ranged from the working class, to the middle class and the educated elite, and to the classless, the unemployed, or the underemployed. No grouping or class has produced more progressive cadre than any other and the answer will remain a secret until history comes forth at a later time with some proof. Right now, it is only important to create the responsible and skilled people who will be capable of helping to organize the masses in their own community. The method of learning becomes very important here. Since the beginning of record keeping, information has been held as a source of power and control. The elite has always directed or limited the education of the masses in general, and of the working class in particular.

Society is structured in such a way as to make most types of education unreachable to the majority of the population. In most cases, the only education available to the masses is intended to develop them into a cohesive workforce ready to serve the interests of the ruling class. Education seems irrelevant to the everyday struggles people have to go through simply to survive, and the result is an increasingly high rate of illiteracy. If people can't see a direct relationship between what's taught in school and the struggle of everyday life, what reason is there for them to attend? The middle class does not have the same relationship with the educational system as do the poor and working classes. Their situation is not, in reality, so much different, but they are allowed into institutions that have a closer relationship with their employment goals and objectives. Most people in the school system are subjected to middle-class goals and values as projected by American culture and history. Thus, when most children come out of school, their primary goal is employment and middle-class status. After all, there are only so many management jobs and so many positions for doctors and lawyers; many children, perhaps as many as ninety percent of high-school graduates end up in so-called "blue collar" jobs. The rewards are high and real for the yuppies, while it seems more rewarding to the youth of the lower-class neighborhoods to drop out of school and involve themselves in some type of illegal activity or to just to start a job as soon as possible. The bottom line is that they will end up in a low-paying job situation anyway, so, in their minds, why go through all the school bullshit to reach the same ends?

Another major factor affecting the education levels of the youth in our communities is the appeal that earning illegal money has. In America, the need for material goods to relate on a peer-to-peer level with other youth, both in and out of school, is probably greater than in any other nation. And for youth in working-class communities, these things are only attainable with money earned through illegal activities. Selling drugs and prostitution seem to be the major money-making avenues for many youth and, obviously, neither of these activities require much education. The illegal money is good and immediate. The effects of these actions on later life isn't really a concern for most youth.

The overall outcome of this lack of relationship between education and employment is the high level of illiteracy in most poor and working-class communities. The levels of illiteracy in the oppressed and minority communities are even higher. The real reflection of this can best be seen in the prison population. There are criminals, crooks, and victims of all class levels and status positions, from upper middle class on down to the groups who have always operated outside the system class-wise and status-wise. Among these groups, you can see the relationship of education even in prison. The vast majority of the population of any American prison tends to be the local minority of that state. In the east, it is the people of African descent; in the west, it is the Native Americans and Latinos; in the southeast it is the Cubans and Hatians. Wherever you look, the education level among the minorities will be lower than among any other group. The issue of the over-Americanization of education is also a factor in many communities. Those of us in the Collective thought an educational program that could speak to the history and specific situation of the group around us would be a particularly useful tool, so we took steps to organize such a program in the penitentiary. The concept was to allow everyone to get involved on an educational level, while bringing in massive support from the community to make the learning process a two-way street. The Brazilian educator Paulo Friere had already popularized a concept that was rapidly expanding around the world; popular education, as he called it, is based on the idea that, when people are given the opportunity to voice their opinions about things they know, the learning process becomes a more positive experience among people (poor and oppressed in general), and they gain the ability to become more assertive in their daily dealings with their community problems and with the struggle for freedom and independence. People need the opportunity to develop an understanding of the world through their own environment and the interaction with their everyday existence. It is only through this type of education process that people feel that they have a voice to speak openly, and to follow their own systems of belief.

We felt we needed to develop a program that would bring prisoners together with people from communities in Baltimore, so that we could collectively address the problems that were affecting us all. This type of interaction also fostered the confidence that many prisoners needed to step forward and voice their thoughts and views on what was affecting them in their daily lives. Just such a program was designed by a progressive librarian, Brenda Vogel. She had collaborated with us over the years to bring some level of consciousness into the Maryland Penitentiary through speakers and other outside guests, and her new program was called "To Say Their Own Words." It would live up to that title in all sorts of ways.

Brenda and a group of her friends spent some time working on getting a grant from the National Endowment for the Humanities to finance the program. They awarded her $250,000 dollars to do a 50-week program that would involve up to 100 prisoners. There would be an internal staff of seven prisoners and an external staff of four outside people. I was selected to coordinate the "inside" staff.

From the very beginning there was a buzz of excitement through-out the prison because the program would include a color camera and VCR, speakers and wireless mics and a sophisticated sound system, and a number of outside guest speakers. These things were always a cause for excitement in the prison. The staff spent the first few weeks interviewing hundreds of men who wanted to take part in the program. There were some requirements for participation in the program; we needed people who would be in the penitentiary for the full length of the program—52 weeks officially, but the program often had additional days added for special programs. Participants needed to have minimal reading skills since there were many books that would be read before the program was completed. After a couple of weeks of these interviews, we selected 110 men to participate.

Brenda began contacting the outside guests who would take part in this program. These guests were "experts" in a variety of fields. There would be over fifty of these speakers and a number of community people from Baltimore and Washington D.C. joining in the group discussions. Some of these speakers and participants came as far as three thousand miles to participate in the program. They gave lectures and discussed subjects of interest to the prison population, with a great deal of attention paid to issues of importance to oppressed people. These lectures would become the focus of several follow-up programs. Every session was taped and recorded on the video equipment, enabling the programs to be used for future debates and discussions in other institutions.

The amount of required reading was rather high but, it could not be helped; the program covered a lot of ground. Each participant had to complete one, sometimes two books per week. The program started out with some very basic books that made for easy reading, and as it moved along, the materials got harder and more complex. Some participants read the required material and then found other related books to consume, while others only completed half the required materials. The books played an important part, but were not the key factor in the development of the program or of consciousness among the prisoners. That would result from the interactions and dialogues that prisoners would have among themselves.

The first session of the program was held in the prison chapel which was large enough to easily hold participants numbering over one hundred. The air was charged with electricity as everyone waited for the first lecture to begin. The program started slow, with the prisoners watching the speaker and the outside guests to gauge their reactions to being in the prison with us. In this type of situation, prisoners also watch each other to check their own behavior in a situation that presents new dynamics. As the speaker finished his lecture and the audience watched and waited warily to see what would happen next, there was total silence. The organizers, those of us who were prisoners, and the others from the outside, wanted to see if the prison participants would take this program and make it their own.

The program was surely doomed to failure if the men inside did not own it, so we all waited. Soon there was one question, and then another and another, and it was not long before the whole place was in an uproar and everyone wanted to get their two cents in. When the time ran out and our inaugural program was over with, no one wanted to leave. In the following weeks, we would see the program spark even greater interest. After each session, a number of the men would hang around in the library area assigned to the program asking questions about the next programs and suggesting ways to make the program work better.

Many of them offered their time and energy to the program, willing to do whatever tasks needed to be done. Since there were always box loads of new books coming in, and we always needed help unloading them, this worked out well. Some men were trained as technicians on old black and white video equipment, so that they would be prepared to learn on the new color equipment. Several were also trained as sound technicians. There was enough equipment for a full production studio. This helped to increase interest in the program because a number of prisoners wanted to learn skills that would lead to future employment possibilities.

The comprehensive nature of this program allowed a number of semi-skilled para-professionals to be educated in many areas of programming. Camera crews were soon trained because the equipment would remain in the prison after the program ended. That would also allow for the production of other programs under the control and direction of the prisoners. The sound system was state of the art for that time; it included mixing boards and shotgun mikes. Some of the prisoners who developed skills would later became sound technicians for the entire prison system.

The program served to develop a significantly large population of readers in the prison, increasing the number of requests for library books and materials tenfold. This was the first time that a program had been able to engage a large segment of the prison population in a long term project. Up to that point no program (officially) had lasted that long. Most programs would suffer from the prisoner's lack of interest and simply fade out within a few months of inception. This program went the full year's time and was missed by its participants once it was over with.

In fact, there would be attempts to develop a number of programs along the same lines as the original one. As the men in the prison began to feel ownership of this program, a collective consciousness developed. They discussed strategies to improve prison conditions, raise political awareness and consciousness among the population. Participants were scrambling to put their thoughts into action, so much so that on some nights the speaker and subject would be completely ignored while the group debated their own topic. These spontaneous discussions were sometimes prompted by recent occurrences in the prison, but it could be something in the news that caught someone's attention, or something that just came up during the discussion that very night. On the nights when this happened, the speaker would either get involved with the group or he or she would be left completely out of what was going on.

There were always anywhere from seven to ten people from the outside community at each program. In most cases, these guests would always get involved no matter what direction the program took. Throughout the duration of this program, very few discussions were actually sidetracked in this manner, but when this did occur, it was a learning experience for all involved. The guests and speakers left with a new understanding of prisoners and the reality of imprisonment in general. The debates that took place during the programs got so hot and heavy that prisoners filed out of the programs with debates still raging, and the outside people left by another door in heated discussions. Prisoners continued the discussion down in their housing areas for hours after the program was over with.

This demonstrated the degree to which the prisoners were involved and interested to those of us who helped organize "To Say Their Own Words."

Those of us who were program staff always stayed behind after the sessions. We would proceed to clean the area and collect the equipment; it was always returned to the library for safekeeping. Once everything was packed and the area was cleaned we would still have some time before we were forced to return to the prison housing areas. This led to a number of rap sessions developing between us and the outside participants because the outside guests could not leave the prison until all the prisoners were accounted for back in the housing areas. The wait for the count to clear sometimes took as long as forty-five minutes and we would talk the whole time. Even as the outside people were going out the door to leave, there would still be a lively debate going all the way up until the time the door closed and cut off any further communication.

Sometimes we would spend our time trying to find out how those outside participants felt about that evening's program, or a previous session. They offered some of the best feedback about the sessions before they left. Many of us wanted to know how they felt about coming into a prison before the program, and what their feelings were after the interaction with the prisoners. Some deep and profound changes took place in the space of two hours, resulting in lasting friendships and long-term ties between those of us inside and the outside guests. It was these occasions that we valued most because, for a few brief minutes, it seemed that we were not in the prison. The whole program created that feeling but it was best felt during the time there was nothing to do but linger with our guests while waiting to return to the depressing conditions we still lived under. We hated for these times to end, because it was the one time we had some control over our own lives. We could exchange ideas freely and didn't need to act in a guarded manner as we would have had to down in the prison population area.

Because prisoners were always being transferred to other prisons, or placed on lockup, and some were going home at their release time, the program suffered some turnover. The number of participants was always slipping down to ninety or so, and new people had to be added. The new participants often lacked the background and collective experiences of the other group members. Nevertheless, we used the long waiting list of prisoners we had, and basically just rolled with the newcomers until they caught up and settled in. Those prisoners who were unable to get into the program because of size restraints from the administration, were allowed to participate in all other activities we organized in the library related to the main program. These auxiliary programs allowed the extra prisoners on the waiting list to feel like they were a part of the program.

Many guest speakers from the program made commitments to come in and help us with the various activities that we had decided upon during the discussions. The brothers who felt strongest about this or that issue would come up in the library and get others involved in the planning and development of their projects. Usually three or four speakers who had made commitments would come in and a project would be born. One example of this is the case of a philosophy professor at Morgan State University. The debate was so hot on the night of his program that he promised to come back and teach some courses on philosophy and law.

The prison population felt that academics worked for the dudes with the money and that philosophical concepts were just in place to con us. The debate raged for an entire week, and finally this professor came back and a class was formed and booked full. After all the arrangements were made for a class room and books for the students the class started; it was to last only fifteen sessions but, continued well beyond this time until "To Say Their Own Words" ended. The relationship established between the instructor and the students was a lasting one. In fact, the interaction between them was so deep that both sides changed as a result of this encounter. Some of the prisoners became serious philosophy students and the professor became a member of the Moorish Science Temple.

On another night, an equally interesting situation arose. The program was about the use of language and during the course of the discussion it was pointed out that oppressed people very rarely know a second language. The language used by the oppressors in most cases is similar, universal even. There was a keen interest in the use of language, and concern about the lack of any second language skills among the over one hundred men there that night. That evening, we agreed to see if we could find a language we could all learn and use. Since there were a number of Central American prisoners coming into the system, we thought that we would be well served by learning Spanish. Some were there because of the increasing drug traffic and others were political refugees. These prisoners were not a large population, but they were coming in significant numbers and grouping up among themselves. They could speak openly about anything they wanted to and we did not understand them.

The brothers who were interested in the politics of oppression believed that that they could use the language to help them with their ties and connections to progressive Latin American elements, while the criminal minded brothers thought that this language would help them with their future drug deals. Whatever the motivation, a class was agreed upon and about a dozen students signed up to learn Spanish. This was an ad-hoc class, meaning that we used whatever books we could find and whatever space we could slip into from week to week. Finally, Brenda Vogel saw that we were serious about learning a second language and she brought us some books and gave us a regular meeting time and space. This was a case where the brothers started something they thought would be beneficial to their development and so they ran with it. The other people in the program saw it happening and joined in to support it. The class was a success and a number of brothers did learn to speak Spanish.

Many of our programs touched on the effects of slavery on people of African descent and the impact that it must have on the behavior of many of the prisoners across the nation. People of African descent were becoming the majority in U.S. prisons and we all believed that slavery played a role in our lives in the present. The lack of economic opportunity and an education that was culturally relevant, combined with the trauma of slavery lent easily to behavior that led to imprisonment. It was a set up for every hungry person in our community. We learned that under the Thirteenth Amendment we were still subjected to the legal conditions of slavery. How could that be possible in the late twentieth century in the land of the free? Ironically, we had been telling people all along that we were being treated like slaves and they thought we were simply being extreme. We were serious but, we had no idea that this treatment was permitted under the Constitution.

The facts are that there was a small movement of people organizing to repeal that provision in the amendment. The Center Against Prisoner Slavery (CAPS) was an east coast organization working on this effort. Members of our program soon made contact with people from that organization and invited them to come and speak to the group. We investigated their work and what other prisoners were doing to aid their efforts. There were mixed reactions to their work since it seemed impossible to get an amendment repealed. Thirty-five states would have to agree and the effort was only under way in about a dozen states at that point. Nevertheless a small group of us decided to work with the CAPS people and we made up petitions and had everyone in the population sign them.

We sent petitions to some of our supporters outside and gathered up as many names as possible for the drive. It was a good idea but, just too large a task for us to realistically tackle and be successful with. The one thing that we were sure of is that the amendment never got repealed and the provision is still in effect today and over two million prisoners are still held in slavery in America.

"To Say Their Own Words" was, ultimately, a very positive program and its impact can still be felt throughout the prison system. The ties that developed between prisoners and community members were strong and lasting. The library was able to continue to present programs for the prison population following the lines of our original project, using the video cameras and sound equipment as needed. These offshoots of "To Say Their Own Words" would eventually become system-wide programs. An excellent example is the Black History programming initiative. Once the prisoners had begun to talk about things that related to themselves, it wasn't long before an attempt was made to gain an understanding of their history. First, a program on Malcolm X was held; then a program on black women who had made an impact on US history, such as Sojourner Truth and Harriet Tubman, took place. These were followed by lectures and programs on the slave trade and Africa, and eventually a celebration of Kwanzaa. Finally, it was decided that we would do a series of programs for Black History month.

By the early 1980s, it seemed as though every community was trying to do some type of programming for Black History month. The public school systems in most major urban areas, especially those with a majority black population, had already begun to make the programs a part of their yearly curriculum. Prisons were the last institutions to sponsor these programs but once we got started, we were on a roll. We had a big task before us, since we had to rely on the people from the community to aid us in programming. We had a strong supporter on the outside who contacted people from all areas of the community and got them to commit to doing at least one Black History program for the prison. We soon developed a small group of community people who continued to work to get local community leaders and noted black educators in to do lectures on the subjects they thought we could use more information on.

The most active prisoners in the penitentiary worked on these initiatives and soon a crew developed that worked on nothing but the arrangements for the programs: contacting people, setting up equipment, doing PR work, and processing the paper work needed to get people into the prison. Before long, the programs had become a regular part of the prison's activities. Participants looked forward to the sessions on a monthly basis. The month of February was soon heralded throughout the prison system as a time to focus on Black History programs. We also developed a video program that taped the weekly events and played them back during the week for other prisoners who failed to attend the originals, because of the limited number of people allowed in the areas at any time. Our first year of programming was so successful that we won the support of the educational department for the second year's programs. The teaching staff got involved and many more community leaders traveled into the prison to interact with the population through lectures and debates, exchanging viewpoints and getting to understand the need for strong community/ prison involvement in order to really develop a sense of community with the local community leaders and activists.

And the two groups were drawing closer together. In fact, you could see the impact of these programs by watching the effects that had on the general population. At first, the prisoners would stand around the yard as the outside guest came in and for the most part they viewed these people as part of the enemy, as were all members of society. They were viewed as someone to be preyed upon if given the opportunity. To many prisoners, everyone outside the immediate family and circle of friends was fair game in his efforts to gain the things he wanted out of life. So these outside strangers were not viewed as friends or even someone they wanted to get to know, except perhaps to prey upon them for material gains. No one had ever come to the prison in the past for any reason that was in the interest of the prisoners without pay or some type of reward. These new people were coming in for no other reason than they shared a real concern for the well-being of the prisoners, but most of the men were just watching them for some sign of hostility. And, as you might expect, most prisoners are very bitter about the level of isolation that they are placed in. They think that society sees them as the scum of the earth, and doesn't want to be around them; so they, in turn, react the same way to people from the outside. They would come up to the programs and listen to the speaker very quietly. They would hear different people make commitments to return and do this or do that the next time. And they wouldn't believe a word of it. But when those speakers then came back and kept their word, it was a whole new experience for the prisoners to have someone make a commitment to them and follow up by keeping it. Once the speakers started to talk about the things that were affecting their community and the prison system together and suggested that the prisoners and the outside community should work closer together and address these issues collectively, the feelings started to warm up between them. Many of the things we talked about were the things that no one had ever taken the time to talk to prisoners about, things like the need to develop programs for newly-freed prisoners, to give them time to get themselves oriented and economically situated before being forced to make choices that could affect their future. Things like six months worth of unemployment benefits. Things like more community houses for outreach programs and stronger community interaction between the two groups. The hard part of this was the need for the prisoners to start working in the interest of the community to aid in the control of the rising crime rate.

There were already programs being developed between the prisoners and community along these lines. The seven-step "Turn Around" program was one of them. Many youth from the surrounding community would come into the prison to participate in the "scared straight" program known simply as "Project T." Members of the Collective would talk to these youth about the real conditions of the prison and the relationships that new prisoners find themselves in. The sessions would be very serious, and all too many times the hard facts would be too much for some of the youth. The group would take a tour through the prison, mainly in the nicer areas, and during the process they would get locked in the cells and left there for a period of time. The group would return to the program area and continue their interaction around what they'd seen and how they felt about it. The program seemed to help some of the youth, but it wasn't as effective as the ten-week counseling program established later that provided almost three months of group and individual interactions, allowing close relationships to develop between the youth and their counselors.

Chapter Twelve

Civic Awareness and Famous Amos

Project T was a one-off program that largely failed. It was aimed at youth of African descent who were already on the path to incarceration, but it seemed to have the most impact on the few white youth from middle-class neighborhoods who participated. It was quickly discontinued, but prisoners continued to look for ways they could serve the community and, in turn, receive the community's help and support. As more community people came into the prison, the network continued to grow and become strong.

There was a pattern to these programs: during the first few months of any new initiative, only a small number of prisoners would participate. But then, before we knew it, more and more men would get involved. Eventually, as the programs and outside participants became popular, the prisoners would meet them in the yard and accompany them to the building where we were meeting, and back across the yard after the program. We were building community with the outside guests, as both guests and prisoners adopted each other, creating an extended family. This mutual acceptance led to the development of a series of civic awareness programs shortly afterward. During the 1982 elections, a number of issues became important to the black community and because of that some attention was created around them in the penitentiary. The first and most important question was: who *were* all these people running for offices? What did they think and feel about the prisoners at the penitentiary? The people who visited the prisoners found themselves talking more and more about the politics of the coming election. The prisoners for their part were seeking more information about the candidates. They were asking questions that, for the most part, their contacts outside could not answer. In fact, in all too many cases, it was the visitors who accepted and respected the prisoner's opinion about these things, looked at the prisoners as having worldly knowledge and insight into the world of politics. It became clear that the prisoners wanted to play a role in the city and state elections coming up that November. It didn't take long before a committee was formed to invite all the candidates to come and speak in the library to as many of the prisoners in the population as possible.

Many of them accepted this offer, and it wasn't long before the first scheduled speakers arrived and the civic awareness program was off to a rousing start. The interest and concern around some candidates grew to the point where election committees made posters to inform the population about their candidates' positions and the reasons a prisoner should support them. Leaflets were passed around that could be sent home to families or friends in the mail at the next letter-writing time. There was an equal amount of campaigning against the candidates that had taken strong anti-prisoner or negative positions on issues that affected the community in the long run. Some committees went as far as making videos for their candidates and showing them in the library periodically to groups of prisoners who shared an interest in the candidate after reading the literature or talking to supporters.

The amount of activity continued to grow right up to the day of the election. The high point of the whole program was the day that Billy Murphy, the mayoral candidate for Baltimore, came to speak and answer questions in the prison. No one had ever given us that type of respect before and all the prison's officials wanted to attend the program. And although no one believed he could win that year, the hope for having a black mayor in Baltimore was very high, and of great importance to the black population all over the city. In the prison, we felt it was a step in the right direction, and one that we needed if there was ever any hope of correcting some of the problems that kept the black community in its current sad state. We wanted to develop other images of black men for our communities and for the world, images besides the gangster and the criminal that pervaded society at large. There were a good number of us involved in the happenings of the community and concerned about the future of our youth. The level of awareness was at an all-time high in the prison, but so was the growing level of apathy in the community and in the prison.

This was the era of Ronald Reagan, and the feeling that things were just getting worse in the black community was supported by hundreds of declining statistics on the well-being and welfare of minorities in the US. The truth was that the party of the "working class" was fluctuating wildly in its position on the black community's needs and issues. It was all too clear that the Democratic Party was moving far to the right in the hopes of keeping some of its southern supporters and garnering support from whites in major urban areas. We dreamed of a new political arrangement. A black popular political party. This would not be the first of its kind, but it would be the first one in the second half of the twentieth century. The political elements in the prison population thought that this would be a positive move forward for black people in general. We wanted to be a part of this developing movement. The National Black Independence Political Party (NBIPP) was forming in black communities across the country, though it was largely concentrated in major urban areas in the north. We decided to form a chapter in the prison after a number of meetings designed to show the general population the need for such a party among the black prisoners. We invited some of the local party leaders, many of whom we had met during the civic involvement campaign, to come and speak to the population.

Although the election was ultimately a failure for the black candidates, it was a progressive development for the prison. The candidates we met were impressed by the level of interest in the prison and asked some of the national leadership to come and speak with us. Both political and apolitical brothers wanted to get involved in the struggle of the black community. We held a number of meetings after the candidates and other party leaders had come and gone, and decided that we would form a chapter and request official recognition. We would work closely with the Baltimore chapter, and we asked a number of our outside supporters to join in with the local chapter to ensure that it would be more positive and supportive toward prisoners and prison issues. The NBIPP National Headquarters were located in Washington D.C., so we also made contact with the national branch of the party. We started gathering members and organizing meetings and agendas, but there was very real concern at this point about our official recognition and our acceptance in the prison as a legal organization. There were some people still thinking about the massive attacks we had faced when we formed the labor union, and there was a strong contingent of brothers who felt that we needed to be first recognized as a political organization before any real political work was started. Others among us felt that we should move ahead without official approval. We had reached a stalemate—we had two factions that each supported what they thought was the best course of action. The administration never did give us official approval. It is a rule that no institution will sanction its own real opposition in a power struggle for the hearts and minds of the people with whom it interacts. The chapter simply faded away after some internal struggle over the delays, because it lacked the willpower and drive to carry out its programs and policies without the oppressor's authorization.

Everybody had been saying that the literacy rate in the US was lower than it had to be. The Enoch Pratt public libraries in Baltimore were trying to do something about that in our city, and literacy programs were springing up all across America as people tried to help more people gain some control over their lives. The trend soon reached the brothers in the penitentiary. No one could believe the number of prisoners who could not read or write. The truth was that the illiterate prisoner would employ a number of disguises to fool the unaware. Some of these disguises were almost a science. Take the case of the prisoner who would read the newspaper everyday. This brother would listen to the news every night and then all day long would talk about things in the news as if he read them in the newspaper he carried around with him on full display. People never gave it any thought, because you just don't question those kinds of things unless they are pointed out to you. This brother fooled everyone for a number of years before it was discovered that he really could not read at all. Everyone was so shocked that people would keep testing him to see for themselves that this was true.

Members of the Collective knew that a large percentage of the prison population was illiterate—it was no real surprise to anyone. What was surprising was the number of people that were willing to give up their time to aid others in learning to read and write. Our literacy program developed a bit unexpectedly; at one of our other events, we had invited someone from the central library to come in and speak, and she had brought along a co-worker who was active in the library's literacy work.

[handwritten: Organized a reading program at the Pratt Library + Famous Amos to appear + motivate]

As always, during our programs, we encouraged everyone to speak out, and the conversation became heated that day as one of the prisoners began to list all of the things that were wrong in the prisons, including the fact that so many prisoners couldn't even read. And then this prisoner turned to the library worker and yelled at her, asking what she was going to do about it. Well, she said that she would come back in and set up a program that would help prisoners learn to read. And, in turn, she yelled back at the prisoner, "Now what are you going to do?" The die was cast and afterwards we thought we would have at least one meeting to see if anyone was really interested.

The meeting took place about a month later, and a fairly large number of prisoners attended. We set up additional meetings at which we screened films and discussed the finer points of just what would be needed to set up such a program. The screenings and meetings turned into a training program with the people from the Pratt libraries, and eventually they produced a number of prisoners who were ready to start a literacy program in Baltimore and other cities. Famous Amos, the cookie-maker, was supporting the development of literacy programs around the country. We got in contact with him and he agreed to appear at our opening program with some of his famous cookies. The opening event proved to be very important to the future of the program itself. Famous Amos came and brought the cookies and the population turned out in full force. He talked to the brothers about making the millions they always dreamed of making and told them how important it was to know how to read and write, just to handle any amount of money. The one thing about many prisoners, and perhaps this is true about people in general, is that they tend to listen to the millionaires of the world. The program became an overnight success because of Famous Amos. It's true that we had to do the real work on a day-to-day basis to keep the program functioning, but I am sure that we would not have gotten started so well if we hadn't gotten a little help from our friends. Everyone working with the program was motivated to get a friend involved, the readers and non-readers alike. Our sessions were structured in such a manner that a buddy could sit in the program with the non-reader and give him support and even aid, if he wanted to, by going over assignments back in the housing area. This program helped an untold number of prisoners and it became so successful that it eventually developed into its own unofficial GED program.

Chapter Thirteen

The House

Life in the penitentiary was rapidly draining my energy. I spent much of my time just trying to navigate regular daily activities. By this time, a number of old comrades had been released and were back out in the community. The feedback that I was getting wasn't good. Some of the problems that the brothers faced once they were freed were so overwhelming that they were unable to do any serious community organizing. There were other factors also, like the daily struggle for survival, the move away from leftist politics in the 1980s, and the abrupt nationwide swing to the right. These factors made it seem like these brothers were not going to be of any use to the community at large. The times were bad for me as well, because I was confronted with the fact that I, like so many others, had made sacrifices and participated in struggles that now seemed for naught. I had begun to wonder what it had all been for, especially since these comrades seemed unwilling or unable to struggle to make our community better.

I spent a lot of time soul-searching and talking to people from the community about these comrades and their actions, or lack thereof. These were people who had been organizing in the neighborhoods for the past dozen years or so, and were still continuing to work and struggle. I wondered how these sisters and brothers could continue their efforts year after year, yet the comrades who were just coming out of prison seemed to run out of energy within the first two years. The problem seemed to be that community-based organizers were established in the area and had credibility with other community institutions and individuals. The just-released prisoner was not accepted by the community as a positive role model based on his or her political beliefs. In all too many cases, their economic situation was shaky at best. These returning comrades found themselves supporting a lot of beliefs that the community did not agree with or even understand at this point. The lack of an infrastructure to accept these returnees added to the problems that they faced.

Needless to say, at the time all I could see was that a number of ex-prisoners who claimed to have serious political convictions were not dealing with the struggle in the ways that we, from the inside, thought it should be dealt with. Who could we depend upon if our comrades were not able to return to the community and be committed to working for the brothers and sisters in prison as well as in the community? These things seemed even more depressing when we continually heard that this or that ex-comrade had done this or that to negatively impact the community. I became wary of prisoners who, for the most part, seemed to lose all consciousness upon release from prison. It seemed to me that they had been hiding behind the cover of prison oppression to do their time and, once their bit was up, they no longer thought the problems existed and simply spent their time partying and trying to forget the hard times we had experienced together over the years.

Our comrades were not the only prisoners who spent hard times in the prison system with organized groups and then returned to society to forget the struggle and their comrades left behind inside. Almost every group was experiencing the same problem and there was a lot discussion on the causes of this new development. The thing that we could not understand was how these brothers could spend years being beaten and oppressed along with the rest of us and then forget all about it once they were released. The programs and support from the community continued to come from the same elements in the black community and progressive elements of the white community, but didn't grow to encompass the newly-released men.

I was nearing a point in my time when I could not put up with a lot of bullshit from people. I wanted to get out of the penitentiary for a number of reasons. This was my thirteenth year in the prison system and all my friends were going to other prisons or going home. The system itself was overcrowded and I had just finished four years of college. I had done everything humanly possible in the penitentiary and the turnover of the population would require another few years to raise the level of political consciousness to what it had been a few years before all the transfers and the general mood in the US had shifted. I, for one, was not trying to spend any more time working in a setting where I felt my efforts were a waste of time and energy.

The classification department claimed that they had been instructed to get a number of prisoners out of the Maryland Penitentiary and into other institutions, so I decided that this was an ideal time for me to make my move. In more than a decade in the prison system, I had only been in the classification department a handful of times. The system never worked for the prisoners and we basically understood it to be something the officials used to cover their asses with the public and with the budget managers who controlled or questioned where the funds for prisoners' rehabilitation went. The classification system was held up as the tool that reviewed and oversaw all the improvements, or the lack of improvements, in each prisoner's situation. This system rarely, if ever, gave the prisoner a fair shake. And most people knew that it was pointless to go before these people if you had made enemies within the penitentiary's administration.

I surely had more than enough enemies to go around. The fact that the classification department didn't work in the average, non-political case made it that much more unlikely that I would be given any real consideration. After all, I had a lot of time ahead of me and the nature of my case was still very political and very public. The enemies that I had made some years before were now top administration officials, and many of them had made it clear that they held grudges from past conflicts. In fact, there were some who refused to speak to me and who only spoke to me through a third party, and I responded to their behavior in kind.

In order to get official approval for a transfer, each prisoner had to be deemed a non-security risk. Of course, the staff would not mention their personal grudges, but the bias could have an impact on your case if you were in front of one of the old clique members. The only chance that I might have would be if I could get scheduled to go before the classification team while a black official was sitting on the team, or at least a non-clique white official. Since the classification officials were working to get a number of prisoners out of the penitentiary as a result of a lawsuit that had been filed about the overcrowding and general living conditions at the prison and throughout the system, I thought the time was ripe. They were processing transfers largely because the staff had been scheduling prisoners to go before officials who would easily approve of the transfer to other institutions. I made a request to be scheduled for a review.

The classification process takes only a few minutes at best: the prisoner is called into a room for an interview with three panel members. Each prisoner's file has been read and discussed before this meeting, and it is likely that the decision has been made in most cases before the prisoner appears in front of them. The interview becomes little more than a verbal stamp of approval and the decision is almost always supported by the administration officials once it has been made. The key was to get a positive decision from the panel before the interview was conducted. That could be done in a number of ways: one of the panel members would be the prisoner's classification counselor, another was likely to be a state employee who worked within the prison compound, and finally there would be a guard officer. So, you would find the time when the best possible officer is scheduled for the team, and you would know that, along with your classification counselor, there would be two possible votes in your favor. The state employee almost always goes with the decision of the other two persons unless there is a personal reason to oppose.

I was before the team and out of the hearing room in less than thirteen minutes. They had decided to let me go to another prison with lesser security. The papers had to go before the warden for his approval, but that was a process that would take only a few days, in most cases. After the warden, the paperwork would be reviewed by the commissioner's office at the state headquarters for the Department of Corrections. Once reviewed and approved by the DoC, your papers come back you are assigned a new prison to be transferred to. In my case it was the Maryland House of Correction in the Jessup, Maryland prison complex, better known as the "Cut." Once assigned to a new prison facility, you wait. The waiting is almost as hard as the classifying part itself. Week after week drags by and the pressure builds as group after group leaves and you wait for your turn to come.

In my case, the situation was a little worse, since I still had enemies in high places in the administration. They realized that I had gotten around them by planning the transfer and having it followed up on the commissioner level. They did not want to let me out of their control, but they were powerless to stop me at that point without some direct involvement. So the major who controlled the list of who was transferring called me in his office one morning, asked me if I was ready to go, and informed me that I would be on the next trip out on the following Tuesday. It was odd to say the least, because this major had not spoken to me in a number of years, since 1976, and we both knew that we did not like each other, and everyone around us knew it. Well, as it turned out, I didn't leave that next Tuesday, or the next Tuesday after that. The wait grew into a month, and then another month. I was uptight because I knew these people were really trying to fuck with me and get me to blow the transfer. Finally, the day came when I was informed that I would be leaving and to bring all my property down to the central storeroom. I was at the point where I did not believe I was going to get out of that place until I actually left it behind me.

It took hours just to go through all the things that I had gathered over all the years in the pen. I left over half the stuff there and was glad when the rest was finally packed up and boxes sealed to be transferred out to the bus that would be taking us to the Cut. They kept us locked in the storeroom for half the day. All day long, brothers were coming by to bid us farewell and to hope that we would never return to this place again under the same conditions. And suddenly, the bus arrived and it was time to go. It was a cold, dull, rainy day in late November 1983, right after Thanksgiving. The mood was perfect. I have always loved the rain and this day it would seem more meaningful than ever, because I found myself standing in the yard of the penitentiary for the last time. The place was full of memories from the last thirteen years of my life. Just feet away, down in the central part of the upper yard, many major events had taken place that would shape the lives and history of prisoners and the prison struggle in general. There was a fence between me and the bus. The gate opened and we packed our things on the vehicle and prepared to leave. Now all that remained was to drive out the back gate and into the street behind the prison. One last look at the prison brought something home to me. The yards were empty.

Five of us were seated on that seventy-seat bus, and after all these years, I was rolling through the back gate. I thought I would feel happiness, but all I felt was the need to never come back this way again. I don't ever want to see the penitentiary again as a prisoner.

Moving to the Cut was like traveling back in time. While I did my time in the Maryland Penitentiary, I had watched many prisoners get transferred to Jessup. The word among the prison population was that a transfer to the Cut was the best way to get into the work release program, the first step toward a return to the community, if one could make parole. So I was shocked when I entered the yard at Jessup for the first time and found that many prisoners I thought had long since gone home were still there. It was like we had suddenly gone back five years and were huddled around the yard at the penitentiary. Needless to say, my bubble burst, and things went even further downhill from there.

The Maryland House of Corrections had been built to hold seven hundred and fifty prisoners. Imprisoned within this structure were twenty-one hundred men. The prison was nearly a century old and had actually been condemned several times in the last twenty years. Yet it was bursting with black bodies stacked one on top of the other. In order to get to breakfast by eight or nine in the morning, we had to rise at four in the morning. The inhumane conditions at the prison angered me to no end and, as my organizing gene began to kick in, I found myself engaged in a class action lawsuit against the Cut. Old habits are so hard to break.

Some of us helped to organize a committee of prisoners who had access to all areas of the prison. We were soon reporting the various code violations to a legal team comprised of lawyers from the American Civil Liberties Union (ACLU) and the National Prison Project. The violations and complaints ranged from overcrowded conditions to the secret areas of the prison that were used to isolate and beat prisoners to sanitary issues. I know that many people are familiar with the overly romanticized story of the Birdman of Alcatraz, but we had birds and there was very little appreciation for them. They flew overhead as if we were outside. After five years of struggle and many threats to the men who were involved, we won the case. The population was reduced to thirteen hundred, the hidden areas were closed down, and it soon became safe to walk through the prison without the birds shitting on us. Overall, the climate changed as the food and medical care issues were corrected and recreation time became ample.

In fact, the Cut improved so much that soon most of the prisoners in the state prison population were trying to get transferred to this facility. But, not long after the changes were implemented, the gangsters began to gain control of the prison. They were in frequent conflict with the progressive elements, who were actively involving much of the prison population in efforts to develop closer community and family ties. This would be an ongoing struggle for several years, us trying to educate and organize, and the gangsters trying gain power and capitalize through the drug trade.

I had begun to get involved in the implementation of programs once again, which included teaching basic computer skills to men in the population, as well as organizing cultural programs. While I was at the penitentiary I had earned a Bachelor's degree from Coppin State University, and in 2001 I began work on my Master's degree. This final educational goal has been a challenge and, in some circles, I have jokingly become known as the oldest living graduate student.

Throughout my imprisonment, I have been fortunate to be able to meet and work with a variety of people from around the US, and a few from around the world as well. While I was still in the penitentiary, Imam Jamil Abudullah Al Amin, then known as H. Rap Brown was held briefly during the early 1970s, and the Collective organized support during his stay. Sometime after his release in the mid-'80s he retuned to visit and speak with many of us from the population about his new worldview of Islam and revolution. A number of religious leaders have taken the time to visit and provide their support. Activist preacher Kwame Abayomi has long been a friend, and the Reverend Graylan Hagler took the time to come speak to the prison population during one of our Martin Luther King birthday celebrations in 2005. Reverend Frank Reid of Bethel AME Church in Baltimore visited me in 2001 and we shared our respective views about the church's role in rebuilding Baltimore, as well as how he might provide support for my case.

On the cultural front, Haki Madhubuti, the noted author and founder of Third World Press came to the penitentiary at the invitation of the Collective; he spoke about the conditions confronting African Americans in the 1980s. Later, at the Maryland House of Corrections, I participated in a project called the Malcolm X Book Club, and we hosted a number of people including the actors Avery Brooks and Andre Braugher who discussed the movie *Glory* and also presented examples of their theater work to the population. The book club also hosted Asa Gordon, the first African American to work at NASA as a rocket scientist, and writer and historian Asa Hilliard, who gave a lecture entitled "Africa's Early Civilizations," which garnered a lot of participation from the population. Prior to the closure of the Maryland House of Corrections in 2006, I organized a dialogue with Salvadoran peace activist Marta Benavides. She came in and worked with a veteran's group that I was a part of, but what made this session unique was the fact that the men in the veterans group who were all African-descended brought in Latino prisoners from their housing units. Maryland does not have a large Latino population in its prisons *yet*, but this was an attempt at solidarity with these men. Unfortunately, when the prisoners from the House of Corrections were moved throughout the system, we were unable to build on this effort. I have also received encouragement and support from actors Charles Dutton and Ruby Dee, and the late Ossie Davis, who proved to be quiet yet stalwart supporters.

Over the years, I have also received visits from many former BPP comrades. Kathleen Cleaver visited when she came to Baltimore to speak at a fundraiser on my behalf, and we had an interesting dialogue on the issues facing African Americans in the twenty-first century. Bob Brown came through after playing a key role as an organizer of the Million Man March. Bob had also been one of the founding members of the Chicago chapter of the BPP. Malik Rahim, a BPP member from New Orleans, visited to thank the prisoners for their support after Hurricane Katrina, and former Baltimore Panther Paul Coates has been a key supporter and friend for the past forty years. Also memorable, if only because of the spectacle they created, was a visit from David Hilliard and Elaine Brown, both former members of the Central Committee of the BPP. This occurred shortly after the Mario Van Peebles film *Panther* was released. In fact, it was like something out of a Hollywood movie, because even the guards talked about this pair. They claimed that the two had arrived in a limousine and that Brown was wearing a fur coat. David, Elaine, and I talked about aid and support for the freedom of political prisoners, but this meeting of the minds would bear no fruit. The phone number that Hilliard left me turned out to be to a bordello somewhere in Texas. I haven't heard from them since.

For as long as I can remember, someone has always been saying, "You need to meet this person." This statement was soon followed by the declaration that this individual was really serious about our struggle. In my twenties, I would dash off full of energy, hoping that I would find a new comrade, friend, or supporter who was also looking to make the world a better place. Well, by the 1980s, that dash had become a slow and deliberate walk full of cautious regard for the person I was about to meet, merely hoping that they would at least be positive. When I first met Terrance

Johnson, I was in my forties and had two decades behind me as an angry black man. I am sure that all of this colored my first impression of him. However, I am still pretty certain that my image of Terrance Johnson was not far off the mark, but even today, knowing the outcome of his life, I am still conflicted.

He had arrived at the Maryland House of Corrections by way of one of the prisons in Hagerstown. Nearly fifteen years earlier, in 1978, Johnson, then a skinny fourteen-year-old kid, and his brother had been arrested by the Prince George's County police. This police force has always had some notoriety among people of African descent because simple traffic stops have resulted in harassment and the occasional lifeless black body on the side of the road. There is no such thing as a routine traffic stop for most people of African descent because of the prevalence of abuse and brutality that so many have experienced at the hands of the police, therefore flashing lights in the mirror very often strike a nerve. Johnson would later state that he was brutally beaten by officers while in custody. Sometime during that beating, he managed to get a hold of one officer's gun and fired. When the smoke cleared two officers were dead and Johnson was in a state of shock. I, like many other prisoners, took an interest in the campaign that resulted from his case. The case would eventually garner national attention, and I was given hope by the number of activists who were involving themselves in the campaign. The State of Maryland would ultimately be unsuccessful in an attempt to convict this young man on first-degree murder charges. Johnson would eventually be sentenced to twenty-five years as a result of a manslaughter conviction, and he would serve more time than anyone else in the state for such a charge. Many of the activists who were involved in his campaign were people with whom I was acquainted and had worked with in the past. This also made me hopeful that Johnson himself would develop into a politically active and conscious individual.

Upon introduction, I had reached my hand out to Johnson and looked him over through a lens that was shaded with twenty-five years of struggle behind it. I was not happy at what I thought I saw: Johnson came across as arrogant and slick. I had the impression that he was full of himself, but I did understand how this experience could create that behavior in an otherwise innocent young man who had been wrongfully placed in prison. We talked for several minutes and agreed to meet again the following week. I soon found myself asking around about him—his Hagerstown time and his friends. There are few secrets in prison. Someone is always around who knows someone from one of the other prisons. There would be information to be had, everything from the crew an individual hung with, to how that individual walked—alone, mobbed up, straight, sneaky, or dirty.

I was getting mixed feedback on Johnson. On one hand, many people did not care for him because of his apparent conceitedness, but on the other hand, everyone knew his story and felt sorry for him. Terrance Johnson had received a really bad deal at a young age and he was coping with it in perhaps the best way possible for him at the time. The crowd he swung with was into drugs, and though I never saw any evidence of drug use on his part, I did not like the people he surrounded himself with. They were not just into the drugs, but most of them had reps as petty thieves, or they were of the five-and-ten-cent hustler sort. These are the type of individuals who are always trying to get that next shot of dope. I soon found myself faced with a dilemma.

There were a lot of very good people on the outside who were working to win Johnson's release. The campaign, while not extremely successful, was widespread and energetic. Many people of African descent in Maryland and beyond felt that his situation was a grave injustice, and it was. Yet, I sometimes wondered if they knew about Johnson's behavior behind the walls and if it even mattered. I pondered whether I should say something, and I considered whether the information would cause people to end their support of him. Did I owe the comrades and supporters who were working on his behalf an accounting of his behavior and experience in prison, or was correcting the injustice more important than his life behind bars?

I remained quiet because I couldn't shake the belief that what he was doing and the things that he had involved himself in were all a reaction to the hell he'd caught behind his case. Prison is no place to be at any stage in life, but it is an especially cruel environment to come of age in. At the same time, to be a political symbol of sorts is especially burdensome for someone who, aside from understanding the injustice of his own situation, lacked a serious political orientation. To me, the situation had always been bigger than Johnson; historically it was the experience of all oppressed people since first contact. His case also represented a small snapshot of my own experience: the Fraternal Order of Police worked overtime to keep Johnson in prison and under the worst possible conditions, and he had been denied parole four times. I wanted him out because we needed a "win" against those oppressive forces that were abusing the youth in our community. In my thinking, the work being put in on his case was tantamount to resistance, and if this injustice was not corrected it would continue to happen again and again.

I remained hopeful that Johnson would have a chance to redirect his life once released from prison. Sadly, in the back of my head I knew all too well that the things a prisoner does inside are generally the same things that she or he will do outside. Habits are hard to break, and it can be difficult to exorcise the demons of imprisonment once released, but I knew that Johnson deserved a chance to try to make a life beyond the walls. After seventeen years in hell, Terrance Johnson returned to the community, and there was talk of great things—a book or movie, and Howard University School of Law. The book and movie deals never materialized, and instead of Howard, it was the University of the District of Columbia, and soon it was reality. It was not enough to be a man returning from prison after so many years with all the usual problems waiting on him. At every turn Terrance Johnson was regarded as "the cold-blooded cop killer." It also seems as if those folks who had supported Terrance Johnson the political prisoner did not bother to politicize him after his release.

While incarcerated he had pursued his education, and my impression was that he was really quite intelligent. However, Terrance Johnson left prison a man imprisoned as a child, and for all the support that he received, I cannot help but wonder if anyone considered this upon his release. It has been reported that, on his thirty-fourth birthday, Terrance Johnson made a failed attempt to rob a bank in Harford County, Maryland and, when cornered by the police, Johnson supposedly killed himself. However, I believe that Terrance died a slow death that began when the state placed him in an adult prison and kept him there until they could no longer justify it.

There was an "intelligence" network that operated throughout the entire infrastructure in the Maryland House of Corrections. Through this network, I had learned that two operatives had been placed in the prison to investigate the organized crime activities. One of these people was a federal agent who was placed undercover among the population, and the other was an officer from "headquarters" who was posing as a rank and file guard. The target of this investigation was the "godfather" of the criminal organizations in the prison and his immediate underlings. This had no bearing on the work that I was doing at the time, which involved organizing around issues that affected lifers and trying to change criminal justice policies in Annapolis. I set up a meeting with the "godfather," a man I knew personally. We'd had a long history of imprisonment together; he and most of the men who were in leadership in the criminal organizations were serving life sentences. I was unhappy about his lack of concern for issues that were affecting the prison population and more specifically those that were having an impact on the lifers.

Some years prior, a man serving a life sentence was out on work release, one of the few programs that were available to lifers, when he had killed his common law wife and himself in a domestic dispute. The governor at the time, Parris Glendening, in a reactionary move then decided to shut the programs down and return those lifers back to the prison. Immediately after this happened, several of us attempted to hire a lawyer to correct the situation before it became codified. Lifers throughout the system were attempting to raise $25,000 to cover the legal fees, but we were only able to gather $13,000. This shortfall was due largely to the fact that the drug mob was sucking so much money out of the system, while telling prisoners not to support the effort because it was bad for their business. Their hope was to make enough money to get themselves out and they didn't really care about the rest of the lifer population.

As the meeting approached, I was reminded of another conflict that had recently surfaced. Charlie Dugger, a grassroots activist from Baltimore had requested our financial support. Dugger had a van that he used to transport at-risk youth for outings, and it needed some work. He had been coming into the prison to support our programs for years and had worked with young black men in the community for an even longer period. However, by the time Charlie had asked for our help, the Administration and drug mob were controlling where prisoners' funds could go. The funds for prisoners' welfare, which came from the profits earned through the commissary and taking pictures, were supposed to be used by the prisoners to better their conditions or support community programs. So, we requested official support for Charlie's program from these funds. It turned out that the money that could have gone to support

Charlie's efforts had actually been used to sponsor a party for the warden at the request of several members of the drug mob. After this, many of us were so disgusted that we developed our own support fund for outside community programs, like a black Girl Scout troop in West Baltimore.

Despite this history, I knew that I needed to let the "godfather" know what was happening because the impact of the federal government's operation would certainly have an impact on us all. I spent over an hour explaining the situation as I understood it, and suggesting a possible course of action. My main motivation was that some of the young brothers that I had been working with had ties to the drug mob, and none of us wanted them to get caught up in the dragnet. Time passed and no immediate changes were made in the activities of the criminal organizations, so I made another attempt to reach out and warn them by approaching the underlings. Imagine my surprise when they said that they did not even know that they were under investigation. The "godfather" had never told them. Some of these men trusted me and quickly ceased their activities.

As for those who continued, well, many of them were caught up in the ensuing raid. These men were shipped off to other states and several guards were also fired. The Maryland House of Corrections was locked down for several months and all activities and programs came to an immediate halt. It would be nearly three years before we were able to get positive programs started again.

Chapter Fourteen

Free Agent

...the demands two people make upon each other can be crippling and destructive. No matter how much they love each other, the values of our society conspire to add intolerable pressures to a binding relationship.
—Huey P. Newton, *Revolutionary Suicide*

Imprisonment does not end life; it simply makes it more difficult. The cycles that are essential to life continue, as if unaware of the barriers that razor wire presents. Birth, death, and love, all of these things continue uninterrupted because we have no real control over them. While life's joys remain elusive, the pain that most people experience is actually intensified when one resides in a six-by-nine steel cage. Not only have I experienced the birth of my grandchildren from this place; I've watched an *entire generation* of children be born and grow up in the years that have passed since my initial incarceration. Two of my nephews have shared this same address on occasion. The truth is that the complications of life keep right on coming; often it is only the responses that are different. And, sometimes, *not*.

Before I was locked up, I pursued women with the same intensity as any man in his twenties would do. My marriage had become the victim of its own premature existence, and though I was still married, I viewed myself as a free agent, and I participated in my share of gratuitous sex. My freewheeling lifestyle eventually resulted in an unplanned pregnancy for a woman I had been loosely involved with. Well, given the environment at the time, and the fact that men and women alike were enjoying a sexual freedom that had never before existed for us, I didn't believe that this child was mine.

It would be over a decade before I would come to accept this child, Deshawn, as my son; it was really only after he, himself, became a father to twin girls that I would try to establish a stronger relationship with him. The past can never be changed, but we have a say in the future. I have always tried to maintain a relationship with my oldest son, Ronald, who has also made me a grandfather with the birth of his sons, Jenaul and Jabari Marshall Conway. Had circumstances been different, I would certainly have had more children and, over the years, I have mentored many young people, because I believe that this is our best chance as a community to change the conditions that have hampered us for so long.

Prison has the ability to capture the body, much the same way that slavery did, and it is especially important to emphasize the fact that it is the *black* body that is so often caught within this system. This prison odyssey has given me insight into what it must have been like to be a slave. Separation from family and community, along with a sense of powerlessness define the last forty years of my life. Presently in this country there are well over two million people within the prison system who are experiencing this same isolation, and their incarceration is not so much for the purpose of rehabilitation, as it's for the profit of others. Two hundred years ago, these guards would have been slave catchers.

The unavoidable space that exists between me and my loved ones is the harshest of all of the conditions that imprisonment presents. The inevitable criminalization of family and friends who have to contend with visits that include drug-sniffing dogs, inhospitable guards, and metal detectors is yet another. The shifty, sneaky nature of sexual liaisons with your woman, behind open doors, under tables, or simply on the fly, if at all, is still another condition of confinement. This sex is so desperate that there is little of the erotic or sensual left to an act that may involve two people, but as dictated by necessity may be witnessed by several. Neither is it pornographic because we as people of African descent often hold the memory of a past fraught with physical longing and desperation satisfied on the dirt floors of the crowded slave quarters or in the fields beyond the cotton. Then and now, we live our love silently, fearful that openness will make us vulnerable. This is the reality for the imprisoned and the new Underground Railroad. There is no shame in this. Why should we have shame?

The real obscenity lies in the fact that the US is imprisoning an entire nation within itself. Drugs have become the pole that many African-descended people slide up and down daily, only to be saddled with court-appointed lawyers all too eager to dance in the lap of a system that is inherently racist. Pimping is easy when you have four centuries of experience with it.

While my children know me as a father, it is regrettable that they also know me as a prisoner; these bars are as much a part of my identity as curly hair. My younger sisters barely know me at all—and mostly as a prisoner. No matter how free I remain in my spirit, physical imprisonment is still a part of my reality. Yet, I am someone's brother, father, friend, lover, son, and teacher, and no prison can change that. I assume these roles gladly because this is what preserves my humanity. The experience of having family members who are absolute strangers—you know they exist but do not know them—is much like the experience of the auction block. Some may suggest that this fragmentation of community and family is a symptom of modernization, but for me, it is more about the literal barriers, the steel and the concrete, the rural locations of these places of holding, not to mention the economics of making those trips.

The system constantly recreates the experiences of our ancestors. Prisoner, family, and community all seem powerless to change what amounts to a truly destructive system. I can't help but wonder what will be the ultimate cost to these communities, whose residents are already overcome by the post-traumatic stress of slavery and the terror of lynching. And who's going to pay when the bill comes due? These questions remain, yet each individual has dominion over her or his own mind and spirit, as is evidenced by the resistance of our ancestors to the system that enslaved them. In *Soledad Brother*, Brother George Jackson speaks of the individual who is completely unfettered by circumstances, and it is in that spirit that I have remained the *free agent*, that individual who refuses to let prison imprison his mind.

The day I walked into the visiting room at the Maryland Penitentiary and saw my father, I knew that something was wrong. His presence told me that things were out of sorts, because the last time that I had seen him was now more than twenty years prior. That previous visit, now so long ago, had been one that I would never forget, because by day's end my life would be further altered, even more than the barriers and prison walls had already changed me. It had been soon after my sentencing. The day had come, just like the rest for the last two years. The sun rose almost as if it were a burden, and the weight of it brought an oppressive heat into the prison. For me, this had been just another day to get through, knowing full well that I didn't earn the shit that had been heaped onto me. Innocence had been of no consequence to the court; and now, I had the rest of my *natural* life *plus* thirty years to profess it.

Not even the blistering sun could have been more bothersome, or so I thought, until my father showed up to inform me that he could not visit me there ever again. He assured me of his love and support, but said that he could not bear the weight that came with walking into that place. I had a genuine love for my father and he for me, and I understood how hard my imprisonment was on others. Visiting is hard; not only is it difficult to leave when the time comes, but the conditions that loved ones are subjected to can be a strain. Visitors are often treated with suspicion, and sometimes made to feel like criminals. I understood his decision, and over the years my father's absence from my life became … if not *acceptable*, then at least less painful.

In truth, I knew that my father was of a different generation. Dad's generation had been the great-grandchildren of enslaved Africans; they grew up during the Great Depression, and went on to fight the Germans and Japanese during World War II. Men like my father had come back filled with the expectation that life would be different for them and their children, but much like their newly emancipated ancestors, they met racism and rejection, and sometimes the end of a rope. But this did not end their quest for the American Dream. Many of them learned to get along, to get over, and Dad was no different. He settled into a job with the city that allowed him to put food on the table, clothes on our backs, and party on the weekends. Rather than reject the status quo as I would later do, he was becoming a part of it … at least, to the degree that a *colored* man could. Dad sought upward mobility, and I am certain that every time he stepped into the prison he felt the reality of oppression closing in on him. He had spent much of his military stint in the Navy, on Shore Patrol, and his sympathies did not lie on this side of the bars. Injustice and innocence aside, it was difficult for him to reconcile himself to seeing his only son in prison. I believe he was ashamed of my imprisonment as much as some of the descendants of those enslaved Africans had been ashamed of slavery.

Two decades later, when I found myself sitting across from my father once again, I could not be happy because I sensed that there was trouble. His appearance struck me immediately. Never a very big man, he had always been a *thick* man, not this fragile person now sitting before my eyes. I knew instantaneously that he was dying. Had to be. The surprise visit alone had alerted me in ways that words could not. Nothing else would bring him into the prison visiting room. This was, after all, the place that had put a permanent wall between us, between father and son, all those years ago. That is what prisons do: wall off all normal human relationships and interactions, completely changing family structures and personal behavior.

My father sat across from me, his face my face, making me consider my own future. We greeted each other warmly that day, but in the stiff manner of two people who no longer really know one another, yet are connected in ways that are unseen and unspoken. Father and son. I waited, knowing already, even without that closeness, that his very presence represented goodbye. Despite the hopefulness that I felt, and the feeling that so much space was suddenly being filled in, I was looking at a ghost. My father died within the year. I was permitted to attend the funeral. It had been some twenty-three years since I was last uptown, but now I was seeing Baltimore from the grieving eyes of a son whose father had long ago gone missing, from the eyes of a man denied his freedom for two decades. My family buried him, and perhaps a piece of me, for certainly I had lost so much in all that time that we did not see each other.

In my spirit, I felt the loss of my father so deeply that it brought up memories that were not mine exclusively, memories of men, women, and children forced to march over land toward a destiny that held nothing more than an empty yesterday, but guaranteed one thing—that they would never again see those they had left behind. For them there was no care about what tomorrow would bring because their days had been hard enough and the night would be worse. I imagined people exhausted yet unable to sleep. They lay under the stars, minds filled with thoughts of the child pried away from loving arms, the husband or wife who would return from the fields to find a permanent absence, or the parent who would no longer stroke a brow or whisper a word of comfort. The same sky covered them all, and it would be the only thing that kept them connected—the sun, the moon, and the stars. Years later, the loss of my mother would rekindle these thoughts. Disappearances have been an ongoing experience for people of African descent for the last five centuries.

Relationships, you see, are often the one thing that keep prisoners going, yet they are also the one thing that makes them most vulnerable. This is evidenced by the prison administration's use of Family Day as a leveraging tool when they want to implement changes. If the prisoners buck when told they will no longer be allowed to wear "street" clothes, the administration pulls out their trump card: no Family Day. The change is implemented without incident because there is no inclination to resist among this newer generation of captives. In the last few years, I have grown weary of these institutionalized occasions and don't participate, though I still look forward to regular visits with my family and friends.

I have had a few loving relationships with women since my incarceration. These relationships were both functional, in the sense that we were comrades, and some were based on a mutual and long-term friendship. While I was at the Maryland Penitentiary, I entered into a "revolutionary" marriage; this was an arrangement of convenience. I was estranged from my first wife Kay at the time, and with the ever-present threat of being placed on lockdown, I needed someone who could visit me in the event that this occurred. A sister-comrade and I were united for this purpose; the relationship was not consummated, nor was it intimate in an emotional way. She was involved with someone else at the time and so was I. This ruse went on for about a year until the "bride" suddenly up and disappeared.

Sometime in 1975, I entered into a relationship with a woman, that would last into the next decade and this would become my first significant intimate relationship as an adult. Even after the relationship ended, we would remain friends. Though I had previously been married, I had yet to experience anything beyond that adolescent infatuation that always seemed to wane. I had often felt guilty about how I had treated Kay when we were together. When she was pregnant with Ronald, she would come across town to visit me and I would not even bother to see her safely home at night. Yet, I know that I was not very different from many other young men my age. I was not equipped to handle a serious relationship, nor was I willing to commit.

This new relationship was different, perhaps because of the seriousness of my situation, but also because I was more mature and open than I had been while with Kay, though still not enough to let myself go entirely.

That kind of openness would not come for many more years, and until that time, I would frequently find myself entering into relationships simply to maintain some level of humanity. I didn't invest myself emotionally in these relationships, and while it would be easy to say this was a result of my imprisonment that would not be completely true. Before I met Kay, I had fallen for a young woman who promptly broke my heart, and this experience would color my relationships for some time to come. I simply did not trust anyone enough to open up, and this, coupled with the vulnerability that a prisoner experiences, made it difficult to let go and love freely. Yet, in the early eighties, I began another relationship and, even though I knew going in that I could not give my heart, I agreed to this situation because it was based largely on a mutual need for support. I had come to a point in my life where I felt consumed by anger, and my new partner had recently gone through the dissolution of a long-term relationship. So we agreed to be there for each other, and though this was a supportive and caring situation, the relationship would eventually end as we simply grew apart.

I have often been alone, but never really lonely, so I can't say that any of these relationships occurred at times when I was especially vulnerable, though incarceration makes one vulnerable in ways that may not always be obvious. I have always been intent upon not becoming too involved because of the understanding that a relationship in this place could leave me even more vulnerable, and I had always been elusive where commitment was concerned anyway. Marriage never actually meant fidelity to me, yet I never used the cover of politics to excuse my dalliances. I simply had not met a woman with whom I could fully commit. It would take two more decades and another relationship to finally break down my resistance.

For over thirty years, I spent my time loving from the distance that time, that is, *prison* time produces, and then one day that space just melted, along with my heart. For the most part, I had passed the years by organizing and working to address issues within the prison, and as a result, my relationships with women had been mostly one-dimensional. However, sometime around the thirty-second year of my imprisonment there occurred a shift in my life. I can't help but believe that it was spiritual in nature because I finally fell in love. This love felt like a reward, compensation for decades of injustice. Only freedom could be sweeter, and though I never thought I would be happy, I have found happiness in the form of a woman I shall call Leah.

I have not felt anything akin to this since I was a lovesick teen pining away over my first love. After years of seeing women who had grown hard through the struggle, I welcomed the feminine presence that Leah presented. It hid a strong will and intelligent mind. Leah is a reluctant warrior who fights a good fight, but one who would rather be somewhere passing out flowers. As in the case of most of my relationships, I prefer not to state her true name to protect her privacy. My case has always generated a certain amount of infamy and, though some people have been attracted to me because of it, Leah is a very private person who shies away from the public eye. So much of my life has been lived publicly because of my imprisonment, that I now relish the thought of having someone in my life who also craves a quiet moment.

Her strength and commitment brought hope back into my life, and with that hope, she introduced me to new experiences. I learned to appreciate the music of Marvin Gaye, especially the song "If I Should Die Tonight," because it summed up my feelings about this woman and our relationship. The part where Marvin asks "how many men have seen their dream come true?" captured my attention: I knew that this was my dream in the flesh. The poetry of Langston Hughes began to spill from my mouth as if I were possessed by the writer himself. Leah and I often have spirited debates about politics and culture while sharing our life's experiences with one another. I am left to wonder how one so young has become so wise, and I'm not afraid to admit that after so many years of mentoring others, I finally found a mentor. Her life has inspired me and I began to concentrate on gaining my freedom again, for this woman caught me at a time when I was beginning to lose sight of it.

I had been struck by the realization that I had always been the driving force behind the campaign for my freedom, telling people I had known for thirty years what to do and how to do it, while feeling like they should have known what to do themselves. It was becoming exhausting and, though I was proud that it had taken so long to exhaust me, I finally threw my hands up and said enough already. This was a constant cycle that I was repeating: reinventing the wheel for political activists who should have known better. When it comes to political prisoner cases, activists and supporters can (and do) walk away and stay away for two or three years only to return as if no time has passed. For the political prisoner, however, it is an additional two or three years of suffering in the belly of the beast.

My time as a political prisoner has also often involved the burden of being a sympathetic ear to people who come into my orbit under the political pretext, but then unload their own tragedies, both real and imagined. I have always been the type of person that people have sought out to discuss their problems and issues, because I am an empathetic individual, but I have perfected the art of remaining emotionally divorced. I listen to people with a critical ear and render advice without taking on the issues of others. I was beginning to feel as if I would never be physically free of prison, but then this woman came from nowhere and opened me up like a vein, and I saw my freedom on the horizon again. Leah not only sparked a new interest in my case, she befriended and encouraged my family.

Where my approach to relationships had been very distant with other women, I was now guilty of thinking in possessive terms. For the first time, I was interested in a relationship and I didn't care if it lasted for a day or a lifetime. What was important to me was that I was experiencing something that I knew would not come my way again, and the pursuit was more important than where I ended up. True love is like that. Other relationships had been about reciprocity—I got something and so did she; the terms were always clear, but I never gave my heart. Nor had I intended to once I had crossed that threshold into this place. But it was as if someone had suddenly held a mirror up and I was confronted with what I had missed by refusing to look into the glass for so long. *What I missed.* I had never let my guard down in any of my relationships. I never opened up and shared my deepest thoughts and desires. I was destined to take so much to the grave, but Leah stepped in and I knew that I had finally found someone who could shoulder some of the burden.

The two of us are spirits that have finally reconnected over time and space, participating in that struggle for freedom that continues into consecutive generations. There is no pretense about it, we both understand our purpose and, in our own ways, work to make a difference in the world. When you understand your destiny, there is very little else to do but meet it. I know that this is the woman with whom I am destined to dance, and that each of us had simply been stepping on the toes of others until finally we crossed one another on the floor.

This relationship presents challenges for me, for no one has ever demanded as much from me as Leah, and she refuses to give in to the *walls* by tempering her demands. It is a beautiful situation because she pushes me to fight for my freedom while providing the motivation for it.

Prisoners tend to avoid depth in their relationships because they make us vulnerable. This became clear to me one day when Leah told me about a situation that had occurred one evening: she had car trouble and it was getting late and she could not reach anyone for assistance. I felt absolutely powerless. Despite the fact that I have been in prison for nearly four decades, I have never really felt an absolute sense of powerlessness before, because I never allowed myself to love like this before. I am not so sure that I am the worse for the loss, because this relationship has opened up wounds that are older than my experience. At the same time, I get through the days on a different sort of rhythm now, no longer dancing the solemn dance of the man alone. Life involves less of the clanging of doors, the shouts from other prisoners, work, food, and other mundane details of day-to-day existence. Instead, it is filled with the sound of her voice, her words on paper, and the knowledge that I have found something that transcends this environment, this time. Freedom is more than a fleeting thought; it is something that I see in my future. While I have spent most of my life in prison, I do not see it ending here.

The last two decades of my imprisonment have been spent organizing programs and mentoring younger men, many of whom will go back into the community. In the early nineties, I found myself in a continual cycle of anger and frustration. I was twenty years into my life sentence when it occurred to me that I had lost two decades of my life. This time had been fraught with the abuse and violence from the guards that go hand in hand with the repression of imprisonment. The stress was beginning to show; I was frequently short-tempered and always disagreeable. Realizing that I was headed for serious trouble, I found support among other prisoners in a therapeutic group setting.

I soon began to realize that I had never grieved for the loss of my physical freedom. I had been in survival mode for twenty years, with little time for reflection, yet I had lost so much and suddenly it was all hitting me at once. Around this time, I was also diagnosed with high blood pressure and this did not come as a surprise, since the everyday life of an African-descended man can be stressful enough. Add to that the experience of imprisonment and you have the makings of a stroke. I knew that this was serious and I had to do something, for I had already seen Jackie

Powell, one of my co-defendants, die in prison. Jackie had died of an angry and busted heart. He had never quite accepted his fate and it kept him mad all the time, until finally it just killed him. I did not want to go that way. I realized that I needed to develop some coping strategies.

By this time, I had read nearly two thousand books, most of them dealing with the experience of African-descended people and struggle. I was rigid and needed to balance my political self. I began to explore religion and also found some relief by reading science-fiction.

I have also been involved in the pursuit of justice for the numerous victims of the FBI's infamous Counter-Intelligence Program. In 2006, I drafted a resolution that was introduced to Congress by Representative Cynthia McKinney (D-GA.); unfortunately she lost her congressional seat, and the resolution never made it beyond the introduction. I also realized that if I am to be free, it will be up to me to make it happen, and in the last few years I have begun to work with my supporters to pursue my freedom more aggressively.

During the past decade, I have had the opportunity to work with Professor Dylan Rodriguez and his students at the University of California-Riverside. I have facilitated lectures on COINTELPRO and the Black Panther Party, in addition to participating in interviews conducted by the students as part of their research. When the pictures of New Orleans residents, stranded on rooftops after the levees broke in August 2005, began to anger members of the prison population, some of us came together to organize a fundraiser. We collected non-perishable items and $1,000 in cash, which is quite significant given that prisoners only make a dollar a day. The money purchased gas cards for the Common Ground Collective, an organization started by former Panther Malik Rahim after Hurricane Katrina.

Organizing is my life's work, and even though I initially balked at becoming a prison organizer, that is where most of my work has been done. Friends and family tell me that I have influenced hundreds of young people, but I don't know. I simply see the error of this society's ways up close and feel compelled to do something about it; I have tried my hardest to avoid getting caught up in the cult of the personality that often develops around political prisoners. I have walked the prison yard and seen admiration in the eyes of others, but had to remind myself, as I straightened my posture, that it is about something bigger than me. Prisons are the place where society dumps those who have become obsolete, and at present there are perhaps no other people who have become more dispensable in this country than African-descended people. The minute that we began to stand up and hold this country accountable for the many wrongs done to us, the prisons began to swell with black women and men. It is as if the entire justice system is a beast that consumes black bodies, and prisons are the belly.

Key point

Epilogue

To be uprooted for destinations unknown is an unpleasant experience at best, one that echoes back to another time and place, where men, women, and children were snatched against their will and delivered as goods into another land. An experience that marked the end of the Maryland House of Corrections reawakened in me that memory that never really sleeps but has long been hidden in my subconscious—what it felt like to be enslaved. It was an experience that, when coupled with what seemed to be a secret lottery in which a few prisoners were selected and disappeared each day, amounted to psychological torture. That torment became a part of the daily routine for thirteen hundred men at the Maryland House of Corrections at Jessup in the late summer of 2006. The following is what I wrote at the time:

Solitary

Each day starts with cups of cold food shoved into our cells. These cells have been locked twenty-four hours a day for forty-five days straight. Twice more before the day is done these cold cups of food will be delivered. For the men who are locked in, there are no visits, no telephones, no religious services, no schools, and no purchases from the prison commissary. Many families do not know what is happening with their loved ones, and the frequent media reports concerning violent incidents at the facility do not help the situation. The hospital is the one exception where movement is concerned: prisoners are receiving their medications. The lockdown has even affected those minor things that so many take for granted—personal hygiene—there is no soap, toothpaste, or deodorant. Most prisoners are only receiving showers twice a week.

Tempers have been flaring; anger seething just below the surface in many of the men. After hours of boredom in their cells, a guard calls for attention from the prisoners. He calls out two, three names, "Moore, Washington, Miller pack up; you are moving." An hour later, as they take away the latest victims, someone asks where they are going. "We don't know, but we will be back tomorrow for more," the guard replies. The rest of the prisoners are reminded of the slave ships that took Africans away. Later that night, most of the prisoners are asleep, however somewhere among the dirty, half-nourished, angry men lurks the dream of payback. Freedom has taken a back seat to revenge; it is a rage borne of this new degree of oppression, and once unleashed it will likely expend itself among the prisoners. Prisoners, like other oppressed people tend to take the anger out on each other. It is a seemingly unending cycle of violence.

"Conway," the guard called my name today and threw bags at me, "pack up, you're moving."

I would eventually end up at the Maryland Correctional Training Center at Hagerstown. The place is cold and mean in the way that the slave pens must have been. The buildings are newer, yet they possess the bad institutional karma incurred from being ill used. The mostly white guard staff is a throwback to a distant time and place, yet they patrol the prison as if there had been no space between the enslavement of Africans and the so-called war on drugs. The fact that this region of the state had been the least accommodating to slavery in Maryland is at odds with the present, yet the poverty of the area makes it dependent on the prison industry. Young African-descended men are the predominant group on the yard and many of them walk around the facility in a trance-like state playing their Gameboys. It makes me think of those stories of the young African children who were reputed to have been lured onto the slave ships with red cloths. The drug game has become the new lure, and it is quickly reeling them into the hold of this new vessel: the criminal justice system.

Prior to landing in this facility, I had been involved in a program at the Maryland House of Corrections that some of us prisoners operated in partnership with the American Friends Service Committee. The Service Committee is a Quaker organization, and I was drawn to it based on the history of The Religious Society of Friends and their involvement in the anti-slavery movement during the nineteenth century. I felt that the AFSC was often on the correct side of many issues, and it was my belief that they were one of the few organizations still doing the work that many of us had begun in the late sixties. So when some members of an AFSC program called the Third World Coalition approached me about supporting me and providing assistance with my case, I asked them to consider working with a broader segment of the prison population.

The Maryland Peace with Justice Program, a program of the AFSC Middle Atlantic Region, soon got involved, and we began organizing sessions that focused on conflict resolution and leadership development with incarcerated veterans. This program began in 2002 and continued up until the closing of the House of Corrections in 2006. The staff at AFSC recognized the value of this type of programming for prisoners and they were committed to carrying it out. Often at the House the tiers would be abuzz after a particularly stimulating session or an inspiring speaker. So when the program was forced to end because of the lockdown and subsequent closure of the House of Corrections, the staff met with then-Secretary of Public Safety, Mary Ann Saar, and she made it possible for them to begin working with those of us from the group who had ended up in MCTC.

Three of us from the original group at the House, Ronald Thomas-Bey, James Hopkins (who we all called Bear), and myself, got together with several other men from the population and developed a mentoring program that would come to be known as "A Friend of a Friend." The name comes from the term that was often used as people were passing through a safe house on the Underground Railroad, and obviously it reflects our relationship to the Quaker organization. The people who have supported and participated in this program from beyond the prison walls have been immensely helpful. I've seen the magic up close. Young men who are initially skeptical or just ambivalent have become focused and committed to change. It not only helps them better navigate conflict but makes them think in a more critical way about issues that affect their communities. Our goal has been to equip these young men to leave prison in a better position emotionally and intellectually than when they came in. Our great hope is that they will contribute to the uplift of the communities that they come from.

I have been happy to see some of these men go back out into their communities and work with youth. They have created a spin-off project, a cafe called Neutral Grounds that runs out of the AFSC offices on York Road in Baltimore, to help sustain them financially. This project also serves as a source of hope for the hundreds of prisoners who participate in A Friend of a Friend. It is something that they all can see—a culmination of the work that has taken place inside. It is our collective prayer for self-determination.

In this place, the older prisoners who demonstrate that they are straightforward and striving to better themselves and their people become father figures. This is a role I have frequently filled, and though it requires a lot of my time and energy, I gladly accept it, because I know that, for many of these young men, a healthy relationship with a father or grandfather has been lacking. There are a number of reasons for this, and perhaps the most obvious from where I sit is the absence created by the burgeoning prison population. Women and men have been disappeared into a system that is unaccommodating of families' needs. The drug trade has passed through generations much like carpentry or bricklaying would have a century ago. I have a godson who found his first positive role model only once he was incarcerated. For anyone who ever bought into the myth that the "bad guys" are behind those bars, let this give them pause. I am surrounded by men who, had it not been for a drug addiction, might otherwise be upstanding members of their communities.

The situational hostility between the various street organizations sometimes lends itself to ironic, if not comedic, episodes within the prison. Here, it is not unusual to see rivals flying their colors from wheelchairs and beefing back and forth. These are individuals who could not readily defend themselves from an attack by a child; men who are suffering a paralysis that is physical in nature as well as cultural, intellectual, and spiritual.

If Maryland were Iraq, then the North Branch Correctional Institute (NBCI) in Cumberland, Maryland would be Abu Ghraib. Located in a very remote area in the western part of the state, this facility is Maryland's newest and most ultra-modern prison. After the scandal at Abu Ghraib, it was revealed that some of the guards who were involved in that situation had previously been staffing prisons in Western Maryland, Pennsylvania, and West Virginia. North Branch had only been open for a couple of years before there were reports of beatings, rebellions, and the death of a prisoner at the hands of guards. So when I woke up one morning and discovered that I was scheduled to be transferred to North Branch for no specific reason, I must admit that I was shocked, even though I had been in the system for three decades at that point and should have been prepared for anything. Besides overcoming my own momentary shock, I had to quell the anger of several prisoners in my housing unit who were mad as hell about my removal. These young brothers wanted to tear the prison up, but I knew that regardless of the cause for this most recent affront upon me, a riot would be used to justify my transfer to North Branch.

So, I packed my belongings and made the two hundred mile trip to North Branch via a Department of Corrections bus. There were nearly two dozen other men from MCTC being transferred that day, and I had a chance to speak with most of them as we traveled to the "new" prison. Everyone on the bus that day felt that they were targeted for some organizing or work that they were doing at the prison, or some label that the guards had arbitrarily applied to them because of their perceived political orientation and/or relationships to other prisoners. For example, one man had a brother who was a gang member, and even though this man was not affiliated, he was seen talking to his brother and he assumed that this resulted in his transfer. Another man was the leader of a large Muslim community, and he had spoken out when another prisoner had been beaten in front of him. Yet another had simply been reading books about the history and culture of people of African descent.

As the bus moved toward North Branch the stories continued, and it made me think about the numerous stories that our ancestors must have shared about their capture as the slave ships carried them toward an unknown destination. I then realized how I had arrived at that particular juncture. I had been spending most of my time working on my Masters thesis for the University of California. Each day, I would gather my books and materials, sit at a table in the recreation area, and work on the paper. In addition to this, I was also mentoring a number of prisoners; helping them prepare for parole and cope with problems they were facing. Often, one or another of these young men would see me seated at this table and come over to discuss a problem or ask a question. I would put my work aside and take some time to address the situation. I suppose the guards found me guilty of two crimes. The first was reading materials about black people, especially the Black Panther Party. My thesis was on BPP political prisoners and these books reflected that topic. The second offense was simply speaking to youthful prisoners, African-descended and white, and answering their questions as well as helping them navigate through the system. The guards actually claim that navigation is their territory, but they hardly ever talk to young prisoners other than to issue instructions and commands.

Now here I was, being shipped off to this place that was hundreds of miles from the city where my family resided. This is sometimes the reward for the man behind bars who educates himself and those around him. Still, I was pissed and ready, willing, and able to fight when I touched ground at North Branch, another angry black man joining the thousand or so already there. The building that we were housed in was being filled to capacity with prisoners from around the state. There was another building that held several hundred men who were locked in their cells all day and all night. The prison employed a portable shower that was pushed down the tier once a day. The windows in the cells were kept closed and each cell faced a wall. The people who are contained within this area cannot see themselves because the mirrors and other utilities are made with dull stainless steel finishes. There is an intercom system built into each cell wall and cameras hang overhead in all areas to record any movement and activity. Privacy is but a vague memory on its way to becoming a long-forgotten concept in that space.

The housing unit in which we had been placed was built the same way, though it was deemed medium security, and many of us were classified that way. The difference for us was that we were allowed out of the cells for yard, recreation room, and to go eat and shower. Each cell was doubled up with two men, and the tier that I was on held over one hundred men; this building had four such tiers. Everything was high tech and prisoners could be locked down in any area at the first sign of trouble simply by the flip of a switch or touch of a button. All around us, above our heads, were control centers with large windows and monitors. Some areas also had one-way glass. Every door was closed, and a prisoner had to approach it and wait for it to open to allow travel to the next door, where the wait began again.

My first day at this facility set the tone for the entire experience. I arrived with all of my property, an accumulation of thirty plus years behind bars, which was then inspected by several guards. Most of it was rejected because so many things were prohibited at this particular prison. I lost hundreds of dollars worth of property: a television, books, tapes, food, pictures, clothes, and many small items that I had collected over the years. Some of the other prisoners said that we could fight for our belongings and they would have to return it in the next three or four months. I resolved right then that my fight would be to get out of North Branch, for there was no real justification for my being placed there to begin with. This place was a twenty-first century concentration camp where the guards, with few exceptions, were hostile and the cells were filling fast with young men and teenagers of African descent, mostly from Baltimore and Prince George's County, Maryland. I witnessed several conflicts with the guards and three of them resulted in the tear-gassing of the tier that I was on.

Immediately following my transfer to North Branch, my sister Cookie and several of my supporters waged a campaign to get me sent back to MCTC along with two other young men who were a part of the mentoring program that I had been involved with. After two weeks or so, I was asked by officials to ask my supporters—who had not only made calls to the Department of Public Safety, but had held a demonstration outside of their offices—to call the campaign off, because I would be sent back to MCTC in Hagerstown. In addition, one of the two young brothers was also sent back. Our other comrade had been placed on lockup when he stood up for another prisoner who was being mistreated by the guards, and because of this, he was not returned. As I left that place after what amounted to a thirty-day stint, I couldn't help but wonder about the men who remained there. Brothers young and old were being stripped of their humanity by the pound. Many of them, and especially the young ones, would return to their communities full of anger and without much hope for the future, nursing a profound sense of loss for something that no human should ever lose. This experience made me extremely grateful for the spiritual soul searching that I had done some thirty years prior.

I always felt out of sync spiritually; the pieces were there, but they were not all together. One of the criticisms often levied at the Panthers is that we lacked a spiritual base to our movement. On the surface this is true, however I always took to heart the quote by Che Guevara that says that the true revolutionary is guided by great feelings of love. We were a revolutionary organization in the throes of removing the shackles of a few hundred years of Western influence and dominance, but at the core was a righteous love for our communities and people. Love, like most emotions, is spirit-based; it possesses us and bends us to its will. In my case, that spirit was seeking freedom for black people, and I have always been bent on that pursuit. However, I have felt at times that my spirit was not fully connected to the universe.

Many of us who were in the Panther party were young people who had come from families that had been Christian since enslavement. I had grown up attending a community church, and beyond the love that I had for the beautiful hymns, it never reached me. The same people who would act as if they were in righteous possession of the spirit on Sunday would allow the toxic gods to inhabit their souls during the rest of the week. I wanted to be connected to a religion that practiced what was preached. So I gave Islam a try, even though my political beliefs and ideologies were in conflict with some of the religious teachings. From 1975 to 1980, I was Sunni Muslim; I took the name Hashim Sal Al Din, which means the sword of the law.

Orthodox Islam had been making an in-road into the Black Liberation Movement because it offered a spiritual connection to some of our closest international allies. Some of our members had been given safe haven by Islamic nations and perhaps were even trained by Islamic groups. They were engaged in a fight against the same Western imperialist forces we were battling and the movement was being flooded with books and materials on the struggles of Islamic nations. On a more personal level, the peaceful air projected by the brothers during Ramadaan and after prayer gatherings was a state of being that I longed to obtain.

I tried to keep my politics and religion in their respective areas, but ultimately these diverse beliefs collided. I found Islam fraught with too many Euro-centric and capitalist beliefs, and I had spent too much time rejecting these harmful tenets to go back. The rejection had cost me my physical freedom; that's how deep my commitments were. The true relationship between Black Africa and the Islamic world was becoming clear as the wars for liberation on the continent did not receive support from the Islamic countries and, in some cases, were met with military opposition. As I studied and learned more about the spread of Islam, I was confronted with the facts: this had resulted in the destruction of many African cultures and societies. It was during this five-year period that I would learn that, just like the Christian church, Islam had its share of "Friday worshippers." While some of us were very serious about our religious practices, there were others who were dealing in heavy drugs, and engaged in other activities that I found unacceptable. Too many problems and not enough rewards; my soul was still unhappy. For three years after I left Islam, I continued to observe the holy days and kept aspects of the religion that

I felt were purifying, but let go of the theological aspects. I became increasingly cynical towards organized religion of any sort, though I always maintained my own connection to the Creator. And I have continued to look toward Africa as I have searched for spiritual enlightenment.

I am currently incarcerated at the Jessup Correctional Institution (JCI) in Jessup, Maryland. I was moved here in July of 2008 after Greg Kane wrote a story for the *Baltimore Sun* about "flagging," a term used when the Department of Corrections has identified an individual as a member of a gang or what they consider a security threat group. While still at the House of Corrections, I had been photographed for the gang "catalogue" even though I have never been a member of any of these organizations. When I inquired why I was being placed in the catalogue, I was told it was because I had been a member of the BPP. Greg Kane's column suggested that some people were being flagged simply because they were attempting to intervene between the various organizations, or because of their political orientation and cultural perspectives, and there was a quote attributed to me. As I have said, nothing remains secret for very long inside of a prison. A week after the column ran, I heard through the prison grapevine that I was going to be moved to JCI. After the move to North Branch, I had kept some things packed and prepared to move at any time. So when they came for me that morning, I was already prepared for the trip. Now I am simply preparing for the day when the trip will be uptown rather than to another institution.

I know that day is coming.

Support AK Press!

AK Press is one of the world's largest and most productive anarchist publishing houses. We're entirely worker-run and democratically managed. We operate without a corporate structure—no boss, no managers, no bullshit. We publish close to twenty books every year, and distribute thousands of other titles published by other like-minded independent presses from around the globe.

The Friends of AK program is a way that you can directly contribute to the continued existence of AK Press, and ensure that we're able to keep publishing great books just like this one! Friends pay a minimum of $25 per month, for a minimum three month period, into our publishing account. In return, Friends automatically receive (for the duration of their membership), as they appear, one free copy of every new AK Press title. They're also entitled to a 20% discount on everything featured in the AK Press Distribution catalog and on the website, on any and every order. You or your organization can even sponsor an entire book if you should so choose!

There's great stuff in the works—so sign up now to become a Friend of AK Press, and let the presses roll!

Won't you be our friend? Email friendsofak@akpress.org for more info, or visit the Friends of AK Press website: http://www.akpress.org/programs/friendsofak